THE UNLUCKY FAMILY

THE UNLUCKY FAMILY

Mrs Henry de la Pasture

Introduced by
Auberon Waugh

Illustrated by
John Lawrence

THE BOYDELL PRESS

Published 1987 by The Boydell Press
an imprint of Boydell & Brewer Ltd
PO Box 9, Woodbridge, Suffolk IP12 3DF

ISBN 0 85115 481 6

Printed in Great Britain by
St Edmundsbury Press, Bury St Edmunds, Suffolk

CONTENTS

INTRODUCTION

Mrs Henry de la Pasture was born Elizabeth Bonham, daughter of Edward Bonham sometime H.M. Consul in Calais, and great-grand-daughter of Sir Samuel Bonham, a colonial administrator who was created baronet on his retirement. Her first husband was Count Henry de la Pasture, third son of a gentleman who described himself as the fourteenth Count and third Marquis de la Pasture, of an *emigré* French noble family settled in England after the Revolution. She had two daughters of which the elder, Edmée Elizabeth, achieved considerable success as a novelist, writing under the name of E. M. Delafield. The daughter is chiefly remembered nowadays for her *Diary of a Provincial Lady* which first appeared in Lady Rhondda's *Time and Tide* in 1931.

Although much has been written about E. M. Delafield, practically nothing has been written about her mother who wrote many novels and plays at the beginning of this century; nor does the daughter mention her mother in her own *Who's Who* entry. Mrs de la Pasture's first husband's home was Llandogo Priory, Monmouthshire, and it seems possible that it was the translation from her father's retirement home in Bramling, Kent, to the different circumstances of Llandogo Priory which inspired the Chubbs' move from Crystal Palace to Finch Hall in *The Unlucky Family*.

This first husband died in 1908. Two years later she married Sir Hugh Clifford, G.C.M.G., an immensely distinguished colonial governor. In the course of the next few years, her husband governed the Gold Coast (1912-1919), Nigeria (1919-1925), Ceylon (1925-1927) and the Malay States with Borneo from 1927 until 1929 when he resigned, as he explains rather oddly in *Who's Who*, 'owing to Lady Clifford's serious illness'.

In fact Lady Clifford (Mrs Henry de la Pasture) lived another sixteen years, dying on 30 October, 1945, four years after her husband and two years after her elder daughter. She has male descendants surviving in Canada under the name of Truelove but I have been unable to discover what happened to the younger daughter.

After Sir Hugh died at seventy-five in 1941, the *Dictionary of National Biography* wrote of him that 'Clifford's forceful but never dictatorial personality won him the respect and confidence of all races, even when the onset of cyclical insanity led to eccentricities of behaviour'.

Until somebody writes a biography of Mrs Henry de la Pasture we can only guess about her life as daughter of the Consul in Calais, chatelaine of Llandogo and then governor's lady in various inhospitable climates with a husband whose eccentricities of behaviour eventually resolved into madness. She was created C.B.E. in 1918, more probably for her staunch conduct in the Gold Coast than for her services to literature, which remain largely unrecognised to this day, although the King commanded a special performance of her play, *Peter's Mother*, at Sandringham in 1906.

In her biography in *Who's Who* she gives 1907 as the date of publication for *The Unlucky Family* (it was published in November of that year by Smith, Elder & Co.) although the Oxford University Press considers it first published in 1913. At the end of the book she seems to promise a sequel, but so far as I have been able to discover this promise was never fulfilled. My father, the writer Evelyn Waugh, who rediscovered *The Unlucky Family* by chance in 1950 and was as much delighted by it as were his older children, instituted a search but came up with nothing. Perhaps, like the Finch family treasure, a mouldering manuscript is waiting to be unearthed in Canada or in some second-hand bookshop. I certainly hope so, but this masterpiece would appear to be the last thing she wrote, although she lived another thirty-two years. The search revealed nothing among her published writings to compare with *The Unlucky Family* which must surely be recognised, eventually, as one of the great classics of its *genre* to be put on the same shelf as *Diary of a Nobody*, *The Young Visiters*, and *Cautionary Verses*.

The author's second husband, Hugh Clifford – a friend of Joseph Conrad – came from an old Catholic family. It seems probable that her first husband, too, was a Roman Catholic. This may explain the absence of any Canon Chasuble or Dr Proudie as Bishop of Pontypool. Almost any other novelist would surely have been tempted to introduce a comic clergyman, probably in

place of the Mayor. But Finch Hall has no chaplain, nor even
any clerical callers. It may seem strange that the first caller at
Finch Hall once the Chubbs had moved in should be the Mayor
of neighbouring Burridge. Mayors did not feature largely in the
life of country houses at this time, unless I am much mistaken, and
although the Mayor is an amiable enough character, and very
useful with policemen when Greedy George is caught stealing
peaches at the Flower Show, his presence might seem to suggest
that Mrs de la Pasture was slightly less familiar with the world
she was describing than one might otherwise suppose. Other
characters come from the official world – an Admiral, a General –
in which both her father and, in a more exalted way, her second
husband moved. Where the Duke and Duchess of Pontypool
come from is anybody's guess, but Sophia and peppery, kind-
hearted Charlemagne are among the most endearing grandees of
English fiction. It seems to me slightly odd that in a house the
size of Pontypool Castle, and at this time, the Duke would have
had his study on the first or bedroom floor. It is necessary to the
story, of course, so that when Mr Higginbotham, the tutor, with
his swollen, bright blue nose, jumps out of the window in fright
when the Duke accidentally lets off his pistol, there should be
some anxiety about his subsequent fate. But while these sitting
rooms adjoining a dressing room are quite common on the
Continent, they are most unusual in England and I am puzzled to
know what great English house Mrs de la Pasture had in mind.

The most surprising thing about the book, within the context
of its period, is its almost total absence of snobbery. True, there
is an acute social awareness, and nearly all the working-class
characters, with the exception of John the footman, are either
drunk, scatter-brained or disagreeable. John's explanation of why
Mr Higginbotham must eat in his room, after the Duchess's
ministrations to his wasp sting have left him with a bright blue
nose, surely deserves a place in any dictionary of social observance:

'How can you sit at table with a nose like that? The under-
footmen, who isn't used to control theirselves as we are, might be
led to forget their places and burst out laughing. It's enough to
make even a butler smile. . . .'

But there is no sneering at the *nouveau-riche* ineptitudes of
Mr Chubb. He is one of the most sympathetic characters in the

book, and although he gets nearly everything wrong, we love him all the more for it. I am not saying this is unique in English fiction, but I certainly can't think of another English novel where *nouveau-riche* characteristics are thought endearing, let alone one of this period. Snobbish deference to older wealth against newer is to be found even among left-wing writers. Cousin Joseph, we are told in an aside, made all his money in potted lobster although the author does not develop this revelation and I am not sure she had really thought it out. The Finches 'had lived at Finch Hall for a very long time indeed, although there is no indication of how much land went with it. When Mr Chubb, a 'short, stout, good-natured gentleman of fifty (who) went every day to business in the City', inherits via his wife, an ancient home, the contrast is otherwise absolute.

Various assumptions of the period – among them that Mrs Chubb's inheritance is unquestionably her husband's – may seem odd today. In particular, we read that after Greedy George has stolen peaches at the Flower Show, this short, stout, good-natured gentleman of fifty gave him 'a sound whipping and sent him to his room'. In our relaxed, anti-disciplinarian society, such punitive measures suggest sexual disorientation, even sadism, in the good-natured Mr Chubb. I can only beg the modern reader to accept that Mrs de la Pasture intended no such aspersion and Mr Chubb's reaction shows nothing more than the comparative hardness of men's hearts at that time. We must remember that the Great War was yet to be fought – the Cliffords spent it in the inhospitable climes of West Africa – and modern awareness yet to dawn. In those unenlightened times, it seemed a perfectly reasonable thing to chastise a boy who stole peaches. One shudders to think of it nowadays, of course. Perhaps Greedy George later joined the Blackshirts and died in prison. More likely, I should think, he joined the Foreign Office or Home Civil Service and became noted for his progressive views.

Others may find it disconcerting that we should be invited to smile at Mrs Chubb's 'delicate constitution', particularly since this 'good-natured lady of thirty-five' who spent much of her time on the sofa at home, had borne her stout husband eleven children in fourteen years. In fact, when the story opens, she is only eleven weeks removed from being delivered of twins. We are not told how many miscarriages she suffered between the births of Tumbling Teddy five years previously, and the twins Jane and Josephus, collectively described as 'it'.

We are never apprised of Mrs Chubb's gynaecological history, nor are we invited to look into her fallopian tubes, as is the modern fashion. Mr Chubb was not only a good-natured gentleman of fifty but also, quite plainly, a passionate gentleman too, and as such deserves a hero's place in any modern pantheon. No wonder Aunt Emily felt that life was passing her by, until she met her gallant cousin, the general.

At least the children had sufficient social conscience to wish to visit the poor with gifts. They soon made the unfashionable discovery that poor folk are seldom as delightful in real life as they may appear in the abstract. One is a virulent teetotaller, the next a drunk, the next two turn out to be thieves. Oh dear. Some readers may even be affronted by the class distinctions at Mrs Chubb's beanfeast although I confess I was not. The arrangements seem to me eminently sensible, and it is only a shame that Careless Charles was left in charge of them.

Mr Chubb has a certain affinity with Daisy Ashford's Mr Salteena – 'I wish we could persuade the Musbury villagers to behave like this', he observes, when the Duke's obsequious lodge-keeper drops him a curtsey – but he is Mr Salteena grown up. No parent of small children can fail to identify with him to a certain extent.

' "Yes my child," said Mr Chubb. "The middle portion of the building dates from the reign of Henry the Eighth."

' "Caroline, in what year did Henry the Eighth ascend the throne?" said Miss Jenkins, who never lost an opportunity of improving her pupils' minds, even at meals.

'Caroline's jaw dropped in dismay, but sharp little Emily replied without a moment's hesitation, "1702."

' "Emily, I am delighted to see that you profit so well by your studies," said Mr Chubb warmly. "Caroline, I blush for you."

'Here Miss Jenkins had a severe fit of coughing.

' "But it wasn't 1702," said Wilful William.

' "I never said it was, William," said his father, with great dignity. "Your little sister cannot at her age be expected to know everything. Her willing spirit makes amends for any trifling inaccuracy of detail." '

It is no longer fashionable, of course, to type-cast characters in this way. But anybody who has grown up in a large family will know how well the labels fit. My own family, in the mean spirit of the times, is much smaller than the Chubbs, and smaller than the family in which I grew up. But among my four children, I have no difficulty whatever in identifying four of the Chubb prototypes: Dreamy Dorothea, Careless Charles, Sharp Little Emily, and Wilful William. Of the four, I have asked Sharp Little Emily to contribute an appreciation of the book which has already delighted four generations of Waughs:

THE UNLUCKY FAMILY

An appreciation by Daisy Waugh, aged 12

Mr and Mrs Chubb have eleven children, the eldest being Dorothea who is fourteen and the youngest Jane and Josephus who are too young to be worth mentioning.

I think Mr Chubb is terribly nice although rather pompous perhaps. He is the image of my father. Mrs Chubb I find dreadfully wet with no character. She doesn't feature much, so I will carry on with the rest of the family.

When the children hear that they are to inherit Finch Hall, their immediate and greedy reaction is to ask for a pocket money rise. Wilful William, who is only eight, takes one step further and complains that his rise is not to his satisfaction. This was unwise for he was immediately sent up to his bedroom (a favourite pastime of Mr Chubb's).

Meddling Matilda is thirteen and does too many officious, bossy things like creeping about the house looking for the key of their Aunt Emily's bedroom so that she can unpack her aunt's suitcase as a surprise.

On the day the children heard of their generous relation, Clumsy Caroline was mending some sheets as a punishment for having broken two plates at lunch that day. I think Clumsy Caroline is the least intelligent of the family. She reminds me of a dull, unromantic, boring girl who used to live in our village and whose name will remain unknown.

Selfish Cissie is nine and her strongest wish is to be taken to London and to have a lot of money spent on her clothes. She tells tales and thinks of virtually nothing but her own appearance.

Sharp Little Emily is generally thought of as the prettiest in the family and I'm afraid she knows it. But one thing in her favour is that she always stands by her brother, Wilful William, who is constantly punished for being ungrateful, argumentative and on the whole thoroughly unpleasant. Consequently she is the favourite sister of Wilful William.

Greedy George disgraces the whole family at a fruit show by stealing some rather juicy-looking peaches, so his father is obliged to take the whole family home feeling horribly embarrassed, ashamed and degraded.

Mr Higginbotham is to be the children's tutor at Finch Hall. While he was staying with the Duke and Duchess of Pontypool he received a rather nasty wasp sting on the nose, consequently he was prevented from dining with the guests. So poor Mr Higginbotham ate in his bedroom.

The last character I find highly amusing is Molly the maid who bursts out laughing every time someone speaks to her.

I think this book is one of the best books that has ever been published. Even when I read it twice through to remind me of certain incidents, I heartily enjoyed its every joke.

AUBERON AND DAISY WAUGH

THE WISHES

Mr and Mrs Thomas Chubb were a worthy couple who lived in
the suburbs of London, and endeavoured to bring up their eleven
children as best they could on a small income.

Mr Chubb, who was a short, stout, good-natured gentleman of
fifty, went every day to business in the City, and Mrs Chubb, who
was a tall, thin, good-natured lady of thirty-five, spent most of her
time on the sofa at home, being of a very delicate constitution.

Her sister, Miss Emily Finch, and Nanny, the children's cross
old nurse, took care of her; and the rest of the household consisted
of Golightly, the butler, who was not always as sober as could

have been wished; and of a nice, cheerful cook named Margery, who with the help of Nanny and Golightly, looked after Molly the housemaid, who did most of the work of the establishment.

The children had a bad habit of giving each other nicknames, but the nicknames were of a descriptive order, so that they sometimes proved useful to strangers, who on hearing them knew at once what manner of children to expect.

Dreamy Dorothea, the eldest girl, was just fourteen, and, being fond of reading and extremely unpractical, left the management of her brothers and sisters to Matilda, who was a year younger, and known as Meddling Matty, a description which suited her exactly.

Next to Matilda came Careless Charles, aged twelve; while Clumsy Caroline, Greedy George, and Selfish Cissie were respectively eleven, ten, and nine years old. After Cissie came Wilful William, who was eight, and sharp little Emily, who was seven. Tumbling Teddy was five, and as the twins, Jane and Josephus, were still in long clothes, their nicknames had not yet been decided upon.

Dorothea had brown hair and brown eyes, and was really the beauty of the family; but she was so sleepy and absent-minded that she often escaped notice; and sharp little Emily was generally considered the prettiest. Sad to say, she was well aware of this fact, and spent many a pleasant hour before her looking-glass. She had a nice little oval pink and white face, large blue eyes, and long golden hair which she persuaded Nanny to put into curl-papers every night of her life, so that she really would have been very pretty indeed had her nose been a little less pointed and her expression less inquisitive.

Matilda was square and solid, Caroline lank and awkward, but Cissie was small for her age, with a nose that turned up in quite a distressing manner; and all three had light grey eyes and dun-coloured hair. Charles was a good-looking boy, with brown hair and brown eyes like Dorothea; George was like Matilda, and William like nobody but himself, being a sturdy little fellow, with rather deep-set eyes of bright blue, very black eyelashes, and a most decided temper of his own. He was in perpetual disgrace, and would have been punished even oftener than he was had it not been for sharp little Emily, who helped him whenever she could, and who was consequently his favourite sister.

As Charles's mother thought him too delicate to go away from home, he was obliged to attend a day-school with his younger brothers, while the girls did lessons with Miss Jenkins, the daily governess; but the brothers and sisters generally spent their half-holidays all together at the Crystal Palace, which was quite close to their father's house.

One Saturday afternoon, however, the children were told that they were to remain indoors, partly because it was raining, and partly because their father had something very particular to say to them; so they all met in the school-room, rather crossly, to discuss the reasons for this prohibition.

'Surely we could have got as far as the Crystal Palace. We have been out on much wetter days than this,' said Dorothea dolefully, for she liked dreaming in the Court of the Alhambra, and sometimes found herself inspired to write short poems upon the prehistoric monsters which decorated the Palace gardens.

'Papa must have something very important to say, or he couldn't take all this time thinking it over,' said Charles.

'Aunt Emily was telegraphed for to come back from her visit, so it may be something exciting. She was all in a flurry at lunch,' said sharp little Emily.

'She was only flurried because she was annoyed. She ate hardly anything,' said George. 'Only one help of vegetables, and nothing else.'

'Why was she annoyed?' asked Charles.

'Simply because I popped into her room and unpacked her box, out of sheer kindness, before she had time to go upstairs and do it herself,' said Meddling Matilda patiently.

'How did you get the key?'

'I found one that fitted in Nanny's key drawer.'

'But you unpacked all the presents she had brought home to surprise us, and we saw them, so of course we weren't surprised,' said Cissie.

'*I* didn't ask you to come poking after me into Aunt Emily's room,' said Matilda. 'If only you had left it to me, all would have been well. It was Caroline's breaking the Venetian glass Aunt Emily brought for Mamma, that made everything go off so badly.'

'Everything always goes off badly with us,' said George gloomily.

'Look at the roly-poly today. Margery couldn't have put a tea-spoonful of jam into it. My helping was just plain white.'

'We're a very unlucky family. I heard Nanny say so one day,' said Caroline.

'Nothing pleasant ever happens to us,' said Dorothea, throwing down her book. 'Here have I been reading a fairy tale, in which a girl finds a wishing-ring and gets everything she wants in the world.'

'I hate fairy tales,' said Charles. 'People get their wishes, and they turn out all wrong, like things do in a nightmare.'

'I wish a real nice solid thing would happen to us,' said Matilda briskly.

'What sort of thing?' said George. '*I* should like this table covered with strawberries and cream, and hardbake and wedding cake, and melons and Turkish delight, and bullseyes and jam puffs, and us spend the whole afternoon eating them. What would you like, Caroline?'

'Oh dear, oh dear,' said Clumsy Caroline, 'I don't know what I should like. I should like to have plates one can't break.'

Poor Caroline was hemming a sheet as a punishment for breaking her dinner-plate twice running.

'What a foolish wish!' said Matilda. 'I should wish to be rich; then it would not matter if you *did* break things, and we could all buy whatever we wanted. What would you have, Charles?'

'A big country place to live in, so that we could never go to that hateful Academy for Young Gentlemen any more,' growled Charles, 'with horses and dogs, and a river to fish in and woods to shoot in, and where we could be out all day instead of being bottled up in a beastly little schoolroom.'

'*You'd* have to go to school,' said Matilda.

'No, I shouldn't.'

'You must learn something.'

'I should have a tutor,' said Charles.

This retort silenced Matilda.

'What would you have, Dorothea?'

'A big library in Charles's house, full of delightful books, and a big garden full of roses; and each of us to have a large room all to ourselves,' said Dorothea. 'I agree with Charles, it's hateful to be so cramped up as we are.'

'William, what do you wish?' cried Emily.

William was busy at his little desk; he had a talent for drawing faces and figures of which he was very proud, and he did not trouble to raise his head.

'I wish to be one of the cleverest men in the world, and the king to knight me when I'm grown up,' he said decidedly.

'And I should like to go to parties, and see lots of people,' said sharp little Emily; 'and then we could have plenty of friends, instead of knowing nobody at all, as we do now.'

'I would like to go to London and have some new clothes, and especially a hat with rosebuds,' said Cissie.

'What's the good of a rosebud hat with a face like yours underneath?' said Charles.

'I'll tell Mamma you said that,' said Cissie, beginning to cry.

'Tell away, Selfish Cissie,' said Charles.

Cissie threw the sofa cushion at him angrily, and Charles caught it in one hand and threw it back; but it missed Cissie, fell on the table where William was drawing, and upset his ink-bottle.

William started up in a rage, and threw the streaming ink-bottle at Charles, who warded it off so smartly that it flew into the fender and was broken to bits, splashing Caroline's sheet on the way.

'Oh dear, oh dear; what will Nanny say?' sobbed Caroline.

'Leave it all to me. I'll get the stain out. I'll sweep up the bits. Get out of my way, children,' cried busy Matilda.

'Charles ought to buy me another inkpot. I bought this with my own money,' said William angrily.

'It was Selfish Cissie's fault,' said Charles. 'Get out your money-box, Cissie; we all know you've got lots of money hoarded up. You can fork out a penny to buy another ink-bottle for William.'

'I don't take money from girls,' said William, clenching his fist at his big brother. 'You teased her, and I'll have *your* penny.'

'You're welcome, if you can find it,' said Charles, yawning. 'Do stop blubbering, Caroline.'

'It's all very well for you, but I shall be punished for spoiling the sheet,' sobbed Caroline.

'Oh, if you would all make a little less noise!' said Dorothea. 'How can I read?'

As she threw down her book for the second time, the door opened and Aunt Emily appeared.

She was a stout, gentle lady, and the children were all very fond of her, though she reproved them, as an aunt should, from morning till night.

'Squabbling again! Oh, children, children!' she said, shaking her head. 'I've come to fetch you all to the drawing-room. Papa is ready to speak to you now.'

'Has he been mugging up his speech all this while?' said Charles. 'I could have done it in half the time.'

'Charles, don't be disrespectful.'

'What's it about?' asked Matilda anxiously.

Caroline burst into tears.

'He's found out I broke the drawing-room clock, though Mamma had it mended so beautifully and promised not to tell.'

'No, no,' said Aunt Emily.

'You're giggling to yourself,' said sharp little Emily. 'It must be something cheerful, then, after all. We're going to the sea-side!'

This event had happened once in the annals of the Chubb family, and the children lived in hopes that it might some day happen again.

'No, no; it's not that, and it's not a cheerful thing – at least, not exactly,' said Aunt Emily, confused. 'Well, well – you must come and hear for yourselves.'

They all hastened upstairs, and found Mrs Chubb on the sofa as usual, with a shawl over her feet and a smelling-bottle in her hand.

Mr Chubb was standing on the hearthrug, looking very nervous and excited.

'Sit down, children,' he said, waving his hand. 'I have something to say to you all.'

They were in such a hurry to hear what their father had to say that they seated themselves where they could and how they could; and poor Caroline, mistaking in her haste the coal-scuttle for the fender stool, sat down in it, tipped it up, and scattered the coals on the carpet.

'It's a most extraordinary thing,' said her father, after he had scolded her well, and shovelled back the coals into the scuttle, while Matilda pinned a newspaper on the back of her sister's frock and placed her on a chair, 'that any little family gathering I propose is always upset in this house by some *contretemps* or another. Stop sniffling, Caroline, or go to bed. You ought to be glad you hurt yourself. It's the least amends you can make for spoiling the hearth-rug. A week ago,' said Mr Chubb warmly, 'a black mark like this on a nice new yellow rug would have been a very serious thing to us – very serious indeed.'

Mrs Chubb put her handkerchief to her eyes and gave a faint sigh.

'You may not have heard, children,' said Mr Chubb, 'of your dear mother's distant cousin, Mr Joseph Finch?' Here Mrs Chubb seemed so much inclined to cry that Mr Chubb hurriedly went on: 'In fact, you *can't* have heard of him, for we ourselves have only become aware that he ever existed through learning that he is no more.'

'Thomas, dear, are you not speaking rather involvedly?' said Mrs Chubb.

'No, my dear. A babe could understand me. You are always inclined to underrate our children's intelligence,' said Mr Chubb. 'Pray let me explain matters in my own way. Poor dear old cousin Finch, children, was a very rich and a very – ahem! – careful man, who lived to be nearly a hundred years old, and who has just died and left all his property to your dear mother for a very odd reason.'

'Thomas, dear, need we tell the children the reason?' said Mrs Chubb gently.

'If we don't, Maria, somebody else will,' said Mr Chubb in a loud whisper which he hoped the children would not hear; 'besides, I like to be open with my little ones. Where was I? Well, children, the reason your poor cousin left his fortune to your Mamma was because, after careful inquiry, he discovered she was the only relative he had in the world whom he had never seen.'

'I'm sure, if I'd known, I'd have gone any distance to see him,' sobbed Mrs Chubb.

'Don't be absurd, my love. If you had, he probably wouldn't have left you a halfpenny,' said Mr Chubb.

'He saw *me*, it appears, in some amateur theatricals,' said Aunt Emily dismally.

'With the worst result,' said Mr Chubb, shaking his head.

'I only came on and sang,' said Aunt Emily.

'He struck you off the list at once,' said Mr Chubb. 'Let this be a lesson to you, children, never to run after your rich relations.'

'I did not even know he *was* my relation,' said poor Aunt Emily.

'They haven't any more rich relations to run after, Thomas,' said Mrs Chubb, weeping; 'and I can't help feeling it's hard upon my sister Emily to get nothing while I get everything.'

'I knew you would divide it with me, Maria,' said Aunt Emily tenderly.

'I could not allow your Cousin Joseph's last wishes to be thus disregarded,' interrupted Mr Chubb in some haste. 'But you can go on living with us, dear Emily, just as you've always done. Though we may be plunged into riches, we shall not forget our old friends. Wherever we live there will always be a crust for you to eat, and a corner of our roof to shelter your slumbers.'

'I should hope there would be something better for me to eat than a crust, Thomas, if you are to be so rich as all this,' said Aunt Emily resentfully. 'And if I am to be sent up into the attics of your fine house, I would prefer to stay where I am,' and she relapsed into tears.

'I was but speaking figuratively, Emily,' said poor Mr Chubb, disconcerted; 'on an occasion like this you would not have me do otherwise, before the children, I hope. You shall have as good a room as anybody else; and, in fact, every one of us can have a good room, for your cousin Joseph has left us his beautiful country house on condition we take up our residence there within a year. As soon as the legal business is settled, therefore, we shall be off, and I am going to give notice at my office in the City immediately. I hope, children, that you will conduct yourselves with steadiness and propriety in this remarkable change of circumstances, and that it will not turn your heads to hear that we are better off than we ever expected to be. You must be calm and collected,' said Mr Chubb excitedly. 'Let us all be calm and collected.'

'If you stamp about the room like that, Thomas, you will set my poor head off aching again, just as it was beginning to get better from the shock,' said Mrs Chubb faintly.

'Children, go downstairs,' said Mr Chubb. 'You are agitating your mother, and I can't have you all crowding round like this.'

'One minute, Papa. About school,' gasped George; 'we boys aren't going to be left behind, are we?'

'Certainly not. For the present, until you get used to – to everything, I must keep you all under my own eye. You will have a tutor.'

'When can we start?' said practical Matilda. 'I can be seeing about the packing at once, if it comes to that.'

'I can be ready tomorrow,' said William.

'So can I,' said sharp little Emily.

'Before I stir from London, Thomas,' said Mrs Chubb firmly, 'I buy new clothes for myself and the children, and I insist on your getting an entirely new outfit for yourself and shaving off your whiskers immediately.'

'My dear, we can't possibly go for some months. We shall have plenty of time to rig ourselves out, and I refuse to make any change in my personal appearance whatever; as long as I live I shall cling to my whiskers. Do not, Maria, let me have to suspect that this good fortune has turned your brain. Besides, we mustn't be too extravagant all at once,' said Mr Chubb. 'We must get used to spending money by degrees. It takes a little practice.'

'I should like to begin practising tomorrow,' said Charles thoughtfully. 'Wouldn't it be as well to start giving us a little pocket money now, father?'

'I have already thought of that, my dear boy,' said Mr Chubb, feeling in his pocket. 'I have talked it over with your mother, and decided to give you an allowance in proportion to your ages. Dorothea, Matilda, and you can have a shilling a week; Caroline, George, and Cissie, sixpence; and William and Emily, threepence – and here it is.'

As none of the children had ever had more than a penny a week, they were naturally delighted with their father's generosity, except William, who said at once that it was a very unfair division, and that if Dorothea was to have a shilling for being fourteen, he ought to get sixpence for being eight; and though he was immediately sent to bed for his ingratitude, he refused to acknowledge that he was wrong, or to accept Emily's threepenny bit, which she secretly offered to him to make up the difference.

Poor William thus did not hear the description of Finch Hall, which their papa now gave the children; for he had interviewed the family lawyer and heard all about it.

'It is a large house standing in a park; a river, acres of wood, plenty of shooting and fishing, beautiful garden full of fruit and flowers; a big library full of books, hall full of statuary and old armour, and the finest house-linen in the world – no more mending and patching for poor Nanny; a silver dinner service, a French cook who makes delicious pastry; plenty of charming neighbours – in fact, the Duke of Pontypool, our poor cousin's great friend, lives close by, so we have *everything* to be thankful for. And above all, children, be as calm as possible; and don't stay when I tell you not, but go downstairs and let your poor mother have a moment's rest and peace.'

The children needed no second bidding, for they were longing to discuss these wonders among themselves. They rushed down to the school-room, shut the door, and, far from becoming calm, danced about the room with excitement.

'We've all got our wishes!' cried sharp little Emily.

'A big country house, fishing, shooting, horses, dogs, and a tutor instead of going to school!' shouted Charles.

'The dinner service is silver. I couldn't break it if I tried,' gasped Caroline. 'And if there's such wonderful house-linen, this old sheet getting inkstained can't matter so much after all.'

'A French cook, who makes pastry – with jam in it, I hope' – said George, 'and loads of fruit. Grapes and melons and strawberries.'

'The library full of books, the hall full of statues and old armour, and a rose garden to read in – perhaps even a conservatory and a fountain,' said Dorothea, clasping her hands; 'and rooms to ourselves.'

'To be rich and buy all we want,' said Matilda.

'All to go to London and get new clothes!' shrieked Cissie.

'Heaps of nice neighbours who give parties,' squeaked little Emily.

'We all have our wishes except William,' said Caroline, opening her round eyes.

'Serve him right,' said Cissie virtuously, 'for being such a naughty boy.'

'Cissie, you're a mean cat,' said Emily; 'and I believe William will get his wish just as much as the rest of us when the time comes, so there!' And she ran upstairs and stayed with William all the rest of the afternoon, and let him draw as many caricatures of her as ever he chose; while Charles spent the whole of his newly acquired wealth without a moment's delay, and bought his little brother a large ink-bottle to take the place of the one that was broken.

2

THE FIRST CALLERS

By the middle of July the Chubb family were fairly settled at
Finch Hall, and highly delighted they were to find themselves
possessed of such a comfortable and luxurious home.

Their old servants were perhaps a trifle out of place in the very
superior establishment which the late Mr Joseph Finch had
thought proper to maintain; but Mr Chubb had insisted upon
bringing them, and they appeared to be perfectly satisfied with
his arrangements for including them in the household.

'My love,' he had observed to his wife, 'it will now be necessary for you to have a maid. I need hardly point out to you how impossible it is that so rich a woman as you are should brush her own hair or tie her own shoes. The thing would be absurd.'

'So it would, Thomas; you are right, as usual. I will advertise at once for a French maid.'

'Why a *French* maid, Maria?' said Mr Chubb warmly. 'Since neither you nor I can speak a word of the language, it would be very inconvenient, to say the least of it. And I am, besides, determined that riches shall not make us forget our old friends.'

'I am sure I have no wish to forget our old friends, Thomas.'

'Then why should not Molly be your maid, Maria?'

'Molly? She is never fit to be seen, and looks like a maid of all work.'

'That is because she *is* a maid of all work,' argued Mr Chubb. 'When she has double wages and nothing to do but to dress you, she will look very different.'

'Well, if I must, I must,' said poor Mrs Chubb; 'but it will be very uncomfortable for me. Molly breathes so heavily, and has such sticky hands. Besides, among other unpleasant tricks, she bursts out laughing whenever she's spoken to.'

'My love, even the rich must expect a few trials,' said Mr Chubb reproachfully.

'I would rather have Nanny or Margery,' sighed Mrs Chubb.

'Nonsense, my dear. Nanny has enough to do with Teddy and the twins, and I have already decided that Margery is to be the still-room maid, for the still-room maid at Finch Hall is leaving to be married.'

'And pray what is a still-room maid, Thomas?' said Mrs Chubb, alarmed.

'I was careful to inquire her duties, my love. I find she makes tea and coffee, and boils eggs and makes cakes.'

'But that is just what she does here, Thomas. Why not call her the cook and be done with it?'

'Because *here* she has to cook meat and vegetables as well, and at Finch Hall there will be a chef with a number of helpers to do that.'

'Well, Thomas, I am not strong enough to interfere,' said Mrs Chubb dolefully, 'but I am beginning to wish we could stay where we are. I am quite afraid of facing so many strange people in my own house. And what is to become of poor old Golightly?'

'Golightly is to be my private valet.'

'I cannot but think him most unsuitable for the post,' said Mrs Chubb.

'He is, *most* unsuitable,' said Mr Chubb sadly; 'and when I think how he will hinder me from dressing in the morning, falling about with my shaving water, and fumbling my clothes, which I have always kept so neat and tidy – I own my resolution falters. But you see, Maria, how ready I am to sacrifice my personal comfort to my position, and I can only trust you will be the same. Besides, you need not be tormented about the household, my love, for our dear busy little Matilda has already promised me she will take every possible trouble off your shoulders.'

'I could wish at times that Matilda were a little less busy, Thomas. Only last week she washed a grease spot out of my green satin dress to surprise me; and surprised I was, when I put it on, to find a large yellow stain in the middle of the front.'

'Her zeal sometimes outruns her discretion, Maria, I grant,' said Mr Chubb; 'but I am proud of Matilda, for she reminds me strongly of my own family.'

'So she does me, Thomas.'

'And I have decided, Maria, that though we have asked Miss Jenkins to come and live with us, the girls must only do lessons in the morning. In the afternoon they should be free to run about, and above all to sit with you in the drawing-room. Their social education is even more important than their studies. When you have callers, they must all, girls and boys, take it in turns to be present.'

'But that will be very tiring for me, Thomas. How can I make conversation with visitors and look after the children at the same time?'

'Your sister will help you, Maria.'

'Certainly I will help you,' said Aunt Emily; 'and I think it is a very good plan for improving the children's manners, Maria, for, as I have told you times without number, they are little better than savages at present, especially the boys.'

'You will find the boys improve very much with their new tutor, Mr Higginbotham,' said Mr Chubb. 'I went to see him this morning. He lives with his widowed aunt at Putney, and is fond of country pursuits, especially keeping rabbits and white mice, and feeding the chickens; and his aunt assured me that he had never had a bad mark at school, nor been heard to say a cross word in his life; so I engaged him on the spot.'

'I hope he will not break poor Charles's spirit,' said Mrs Chubb.

'I should think it very improbable,' said Mr Chubb rather gloomily.

Matilda was much pleased to hear that she was to help her mamma in entertaining callers at Finch Hall.

'Being in my teens,' she said to Miss Jenkins, 'I consider myself very nearly grown up; and evidently Papa agrees with me, for he said he should always count upon *me*, even if the others only took it in turns to help Mamma. I have always thought Papa understood me better than anyone else.'

'You are a very silly little girl, dear,' said Miss Jenkins, who had an aggravating way of not appearing to notice that Matilda was taller than she was, and always treated her as though she were still a mere child.

As soon as Mrs Chubb was sufficiently recovered from the journey to be at home to visitors, the children were desired to be ready at a moment's notice to come into the drawing-room in the afternoon, and told to sit in the orangery within reach of her call. The orangery was in fact an immense conservatory, opening on one side into a ballroom and on the other into the drawing-room. In a recess was a fernery bounded on three sides by rocks, where a delightful fountain played in a dim green light above a pool full of gold and silver fish.

Here the children assembled. The girls were dressed in white frocks, Careless Charles and Greedy George had their first Eton suits, and Wilful William, to his disgust and fury, was forced into a pretty black velvet tunic and knickerbockers, and had his front lock of hair nicely curled with the tongs, so that it stood up like a crest. He sat down gloomily in a corner of the conservatory, and sharp little Emily sat by his side and tried in vain to console him.

'For a fellow of eight it looks ridiculous,' he said, shedding a tear unseen. 'Why couldn't I have a proper suit like Charles and George?'

'It pleases Mamma to see you look so pretty, William,' said Emily meekly.

'Pretty! How dare you say I look pretty!' said William angrily. 'I'm not a girl. I'll bash my face in with a brick if you say it again.'

'Oh, William, please, please don't!' shrieked Emily, in great terror.

'Well, I've warned you,' said William, secretly pleased to have frightened her so easily.

'I wonder you allow William to make you cry,' said Selfish Cissie, tossing her head. 'Of course he's growling as usual, instead of being thankful for his beautiful velvet clothes.'

'Thankful for fiddlesticks!' said Charles. 'It may please *you*, Cissie, to be a dressed-up doll with a turned-up nose and a nasty little pigtail, but I call it jolly hard on William to be figged out in this way. He looks like a black cockatoo with a yellow crest.'

'Nanny *would* take the tongs to curl his hair, though he begged her not,' said Emily, still weeping.

'Well, he can easily take the curl out; all he's got to do is to kneel down by the fountain and dip his head in,' said Charles cheerfully.

William lost not a moment. He balanced himself on his hands and knees and leant over the ornamental stone edge of the fountain till his face was purple; but the basin was too deep for him.

'I'll help you,' said Charles, and he obligingly lifted his feet off the ground. In went William's head sure enough, but unluckily his weight was more than Charles had expected, and the rest of him followed. Dorothea and Matilda flew to their brothers' assistance, and as Charles still held manfully to William's ankles, they soon pulled him out, choking and spluttering, and laid him on the tesselated pavement of the conservatory.

But alas for the black velvet suit! Poor William was now a sorry object.

'I'd better go to bed,' he gasped. 'I'm sure to be sent there anyway.'

'I didn't do it on purpose, old chap,' said Charles.

'I don't care if you did. I can't wear it again, thank goodness,' said William, with chattering teeth.

'Come at once, or you'll catch your death,' cried busy Matilda, and she seized the dripping William's hands and raced him upstairs to the nursery.

Meanwhile Dreamy Dorothea – who was enchanted with her first really pretty dress, and almost equally pleased with Tennyson's poems, which she had found in the library – forgot the order that she was to stay in the orangery, and stepped out into the garden with her eyes on her book.

Half reading, half chanting, she wandered absently through the park and into the woods. Here, vaguely feeling that the shade was pleasant, she sat down at the foot of a fir tree, and lifted her eyes at last from the printed page.

'It looks like a magic wood – oh that it might be!' said Dorothea dreamily. 'Then I should see a knight wandering down this romantic glade, warbling perchance some ancient ballade as he came; and presently he would fall at my feet, crying aloud . . .'

But before she could decide what the knight should cry, she was startled by the sight of a very round little old gentleman, carrying the tail of what seemed to be a long cloak over his arm, and humming a gay little tune.

He was just as much startled to see Dorothea as she was to see him; in fact, he was so much startled that he forgot to look where he was going, put his foot into a rabbit hole, and tumbled down.

Fortunately the ground was thickly covered with dead leaves and moss, so the little old gentleman was up again in a moment, brushing his knees and looking very much embarrassed.

'I hope you have not hurt yourself,' said Dorothea politely.

'Not at all, thank you,' said the old gentleman. 'But I did not expect to see any one here, this being a private path through the woods.'

'They are *our* woods, so I can't be trespassing,' said Dorothea, rising with some dignity.

'Allow me,' said the old gentleman, assisting her. 'Then you must be one of the new family,' and he bowed. 'I am now on my way to call at Finch Hall. I was a very old friend of the late owner, so I took a short cut through the woods. I am sorry I startled you.'

'Oh, it doesn't matter at all,' said Dorothea, blushing; 'in fact, I was just wishing somebody *would* appear. That is to say – not anybody in the least like *you*, of course, I mean –' She grew more confused because she thought the old gentleman looked rather cross. 'I was reading about King Arthur's Round Table, and wishing I could see a knight,' faltered Dorothea.

'That is very curious,' said the little old gentleman, looking quite pleased again, 'because I *am* a knight.'

'You!' gasped Dorothea. 'You a knight! Impossible!'

'Not at all impossible,' said the old gentleman sharply. 'Let me tell you, young lady, that you see before you the Mayor of Burridge, Sir Jeremy Wandle.'

'I beg your pardon,' said Dorothea, feeling she was expected to apologise.

'I suppose you can't imagine a knight except in a suit of armour,' said Sir Jeremy rather resentfully.

Dorothea could not help thinking he would have found it very difficult to breathe in a suit of armour, being, as he was, such a remarkably stout little gentleman, but she said nothing, and looked so dejected that the Mayor was sorry for her, for he was the most good-natured knight in the world, and he did not know that the poetic maid was already busy turning her disappointment into verse.

'Come, come; I dare say a pretty young lady like you looked for a younger knight than I am,' he said consolingly; 'so if you'll shake hands with your cousin's old friend, he'll take himself off and trouble you no more.'

'Oh, but I'll walk to the house with you,' said Dorothea, suddenly remembering her manners. 'And please, as we walk, do tell me how and why you got knighted, and who generally buckles on your sword and spurs when you are – well, in fuller dress even than you are at present,' she said as delicately as she could.

Sir Jeremy was very pleased to talk about himself, and though Dorothea's attention wandered, he did not discover it, so before they reached the house she had composed and committed to memory:

The Maiden's Lament

One more illusion fled! ah, wretched me!
As in the woods I softly made my moan,
Aye! In the woods, and seated all alone,
He *came. Yet 'twas not he!*

No flashing helmet glowered from his crown,
No dark and war-worn face from visor paled,
And not from stress of wounds his footsteps failed
　　When he fell down!

One more illusion gone! Ah, wretched me!
Where are the knights of old, so lean and lank,
With gloomy eye, fierce smile, and armoured shank?
　　Can this thing be?

She murmured the last line unwittingly aloud, letting her wondering glance rest upon Sir Jeremy's flushed and heated face, just as he was relating that he had once swept out his employer's office – and though he was surprised at her old-fashioned phraseology, he well understood her astonishment.

'Yes, my dear young lady. I assure you it was so, though you would hardly believe it to look at me now,' he said. 'But I must really beg you not to go so fast, for the day is warm, and I get out of breath walking and talking at the same time.'

Dorothea obligingly slackened her pace, and they now walked so slowly that she feared it would be quite late in the evening before they could arrive at the Hall.

In the meantime Mrs Chubb was seated nervously on the drawing-room sofa, waiting for her callers to arrive. She wore a new black satin gown with a lace tippet, and by her side was Aunt Emily in violet silk.

'When the conversation flags, which it is sure to do, as we are so unaccustomed to visitors, I have settled with Thomas that I am to make you a sign, and you must say, "Would you like to see the children?" ' said Mrs Chubb.

'Very well,' said Aunt Emily; 'but suppose they say "No"? What am I to do then?'

'Why, then, of course, you are to do nothing,' said poor Mrs Chubb. 'I wonder Thomas never thought of that. However, I should hope it was very unlikely.'

'I might put it so that they couldn't refuse,' suggested Aunt Emily brightly. 'Suppose I said, "I am *sure* you'd like to see the children," and got up at once and went to fetch them before they had time to contradict me. How would that be?'

'That would do very well; but don't be too sudden in your

movements, for you know I always scream when I'm startled; and don't leave me too long, for you know how unfit I am to entertain anybody all by myself.'

At this moment Admiral and Mrs Plumpton were announced, and Mrs Chubb and Aunt Emily both sprang up to receive them. The children, who were waiting in the orangery, heard the announcement, and at once began to dispute who must be the first to go into the drawing-room.

'As Dorothea has gone, and Matilda's upstairs drying William, I suppose I ought to go,' said Careless Charles sulkily. 'But I'm not going to wait to be fetched. I shall just stroll in as if I didn't know any one was there.'

His brothers and sisters were much awed by his courage, and he set off so decisively that he collided violently in the doorway with Aunt Emily, who, true to her promise, was dashing out of the room to call him, before the Admiral had time to say he didn't like children.

Poor Aunt Emily received such a bump that she was obliged to hurry speechless through the conservatory to her own room, with a handkerchief to her face, after making signs to Charles to go into the drawing-room all the same, which he did, much grieved to have hurt his good aunt. But he came out in triumph shortly afterwards.

'The Admiral's the most decent old beggar I ever saw,' he said. 'Seeing my clothes, he jumped to the conclusion that I was an Eton boy, and tipped me half a sovereign; and when I explained I *wasn't* an Eton boy, he tipped me another for my truthfulness. Then they all began jawing about the twins, and the Admiral's wife wants to see them, so I said I'd tell the girls to fetch them, and hooked it.'

'I'll run and get them,' said sharp little Emily.

'You're too young to carry them,' said Meddling Matilda, who had just come down again. 'I'll take both.'

'They can't really want both – you've only got to say they're just the same, one as another,' said Charles, disgusted.

'I'm next to Matilda, and I think I ought to have my share of the twins,' complained Caroline. 'Why should everybody get sovereigns except me? I want to see the Admiral too. It's not fair!'

'Leave it to me,' said Matilda hastily, for she knew well that when once Caroline began to cry there was no stopping her. 'I'll get both the twins ready, and we'll each take one; only mind you don't drop yours, Caroline. Remember with a baby it's not a question of breaking it, but of killing it.'

'Or of making it an idiot for life,' said Charles warningly, as Caroline and Matilda hurried away. 'Well, I've done my share of entertaining callers for one day, and I'm quite satisfied with the result, so I shall now go out and get a rabbit or two.'

'Where will you get them? Take me with you!' cried Cissie and Emily eagerly.

'Certainly not. I shall take a gun. Girls can't go shooting,' said Charles.

'You'll shoot yourself,' said Cissie crossly.

But just then a carriage was seen coming slowly up the avenue, with a beautifully dressed lady inside, and a very large coachman and an enormous powdered footman on the box.

'Quick, quick, Cissie! Let us run upstairs to the gallery and look over the banisters and watch them arrive,' said sharp little Emily. 'George is there already with a fishing-rod, getting things off the refreshment trays that are being carried into the drawing-room.'

Charles, finding the coast clear, went off quietly into the study and picked up a gun, which he knew to be loaded, because his father, who was not a sportsman himself, had cautioned him against the danger of touching it.

'As I shall be careful not to point it at somebody's head, like fellows in newspapers always do, it can't matter if I take it out,' said Charles. 'I wish the cartridges weren't locked up. However, I can have two shots. It will look well if I come in carrying a couple of rabbits. I must begin, as father says, to be a country gentleman sooner or later, and why not now? I will slip softly through the conservatory and then run for it, or somebody will be sure to see me and stop me.'

This was all very well, but as he slipped softly through the conservatory he carried the gun so carelessly that an overhanging palm caught the trigger, and it went off, just as Clumsy Caroline entered with the first twin and held it up to see the pretty fountain play.

Simultaneously perceiving her careless brother with a gun in his hands, and hearing the explosion, Caroline did not doubt for an instant that she had been shot, and with a piercing shriek of terror she dropped the twin into the fountain and fled from the orangery, screaming at the top of her voice.

Charles, seeing that he had shot clean through the glass-house into the garden, delayed not a moment, but ran like a hare across the lawn and into the woods, that he might yet seize the opportunity of getting one shot upon his own account.

In the drawing-room the shot, the scream, and the crash of breaking glass were all heard at once.

'What can that be?' cried the Admiral.

'One of the children must be killed!' cried poor Mrs Chubb. 'Depend upon it, this is Thomas. He *would* get the gamekeeper to show him how to load a gun this morning, though I begged him not, and this is the result. Oh, Emily, Emily, go and see!'

Poor Aunt Emily – who had but just returned to the drawing-room, with a large piece of plaster upon her already much swollen lip – ran to the door, the Admiral hastened after her, and his wife supported Mrs Chubb's tottering footsteps.

There was no one to be seen.

'I thought I heard a splash,' said the Admiral. 'There seems to be a bundle floating in this basin. Bless me, it's a baby!'

Being quite at home in the water, he put one leg into the fountain, and cautiously waded through the lilies to the middle of the tank, whither the twin had drifted, and where it now lay floating peacefully on its back, staring up at the green light, and blinking when the fountain splashed its face.

'Admiral, Admiral, what can you be doing, deliberately standing in cold water up to your middle? Think of your rheumatics!' cried his wife indignantly. 'And what is that nasty wet bundle you are holding?'

Here the bundle burst into such a loud roar that Aunt Emily fainted away, the poor Admiral nearly dropped it again, and its mother rushed forward and snatched it from him.

'It is one of the twins, either Jane or Josephus, but I cannot at this moment tell you which,' cried Mrs Chubb, distracted. 'Whichever it is, you have saved its life.'

'Pooh, nonsense!' said the gallant Admiral. 'There was no real danger.'

'The Admiral can swim like a fish,' said his wife proudly.

'There wouldn't be room for him to swim in that little fountain,' sobbed Mrs Chubb.

'Admiral, you must change your boots at least, I insist on it,' said his wife, 'while I try and bring this poor thing to,' and she did her best to revive Aunt Emily by seizing a watering-can and sprinkling her face with the contents.

'Well, well, perhaps I had better,' said the Admiral, and he sat on the floor and took off his boots then and there. 'If you're sure the baby isn't shot.'

'How can I be sure?' said poor Mrs Chubb. 'From the way it's screaming I should think it only too likely.'

Mr Chubb now came into the orangery in such an excited frame of mind that he hardly noticed Aunt Emily lying flat on her back in a dead faint, with the Admiral's wife busily watering her face; nor had he time to be astonished that the Admiral himself was sitting on the pavement with his boots off. He only observed that his wife was passionately embracing one of the twins.

'Maria, I beg! Is this a time for fondling your child? I find three visitors in the drawing-room all alone, and left to entertain each other. What can be the meaning of this?'

'Oh, Thomas,' sobbed his wife, 'either Jane or Josephus is shot or drowned, or perhaps both.'

'No, no – the shot evidently broke the glass outwards,' said the intelligent Admiral, pointing at the splintered pane. 'And the child can hardly be much hurt. Look how it's wriggling.'

But Mr Chubb was far too much agitated to listen. 'When I tell you, Maria,' he said, 'that the Duchess of Pontypool is in the drawing-room, seated opposite the two Miss Pitts, whom she doesn't know, and, worse still, whom she evidently doesn't *want* to know, perhaps you'll have the goodness to attend to me.'

'When I tell *you*, Thomas, that the twin was in the fountain, and that this brave man risked his life . . .'

'Come, come,' said the kind Admiral. 'My wife knows the Duchess, and she's the most charitable person in the world, full of good works. She shall go and explain matters to her, while you are good enough to lend me a pair of dry boots. Allow me to introduce myself. I am Admiral Plumpton, one of poor Joseph Finch's oldest friends.'

'Bless me!' said Mr Chubb, recovering himself. 'I am shocked at my own heedlessness. Come to my dressing-room at once. I have several pairs of most expensive boots at your service. Maria, do once for all get rid of that child and go to the Duchess.'

'Leave it all to me, Papa,' said Matilda, entering breathlessly, with the other twin under one arm. 'I have just seen Caroline, and heard what has happened. I'll take Jane (or Josephus) out into the sun, and it will be dry in a moment; and Nanny need never know anything of the matter, for she is having her usual afternoon nap.'

'Pray, who is Nanny?' said the astonished Admiral.

'Our old nurse,' said Mr Chubb. 'She is afflicted, I am sorry to say, with a very violent temper, and we are obliged to conceal these little *contretemps* from her as much as possible. Matilda, my dear useful child, take the twins out and give them a sun bath as you suggest. Nothing like the open-air cure, Admiral.'

'Take my air-cushion, Matilda. The grass may be damp,' said Mrs Chubb anxiously.

'Certainly, Mamma,' said Matilda, and the active child was gone in a moment.

3

FISHING, SHOOTING, AND BOATING

Aunt Emily having now recovered from her faint, the Admiral's wife gave her and the agitated Mrs Chubb each an arm to the drawing-room, while Mr Chubb conducted the Admiral upstairs.

'You appear to have a large family, Mr Chubb,' said the Admiral, who could not help seeing Cissie and Emily scuttle away at his approach.

'Five boys and six girls,' said Mr Chubb, with pride. 'The boys are manly fellows, and I am determined they shall be good sportsmen.'

'Quite right, quite right,' said the Admiral. 'None of your milksops for me. Why, what have we here – a nice little boy with a fishing-rod, eh?'

The fact was that George had become entangled with his line, and being a very fat, slow, and heavy little boy, he found it impossible to get away as quickly as his sisters, so there he stood in a fright, in the gallery, holding his rod, with a basket slung across his shoulders.

'Where did you get that rod, George?' said his father, secretly pleased to see his son look so much like a sportsman already.

'I found it in the study, Papa.'

'Have you been fishing?'

'Yes, Papa.'

'Promising lad, promising lad,' said the Admiral, feeling in his pocket, and discovering to his regret that he had no more half-sovereigns left. 'Let's see what you've caught.'

'Who showed you how, George?' said Mr Chubb anxiously. 'You've not been to the river alone, I hope? You remember I forbade you?'

'I haven't been near the river, Father. I thought I'd better practise on dry land,' said George, looking rather foolish.

Here the Admiral opened the basket and drew out a bunch of grapes.

'Why, this is a queer kind of fish, young man!'

'George, what does this mean? Have you been fishing in the conservatories?' said Mr Chubb sternly.

'No, Father. I leant over the banisters and hooked it off the fruit dish which Golightly was carrying into the drawing-room,' faltered George.

'Shall I never cure you of this disgusting habit of prowling after food like a wild beast, sir?' thundered Mr Chubb. 'Put down the rod and basket, and go to bed! I was just about to send you down to the drawing-room to see the Duchess of Pontypool, and to partake of the refreshments that will presently be carried to her. But you deserve no such privilege. Your younger brother shall go in your stead. Send William, sir.'

'William's not dressed, and Nanny's asleep,' said George sulkily.

'Then wake her at your peril, sir! Dressed or not dressed, William takes your place. Don't argue, but tell him to go down at once just as he is, and put yourself to bed instantly. Prompt obedience is my motto, George, as you know very well; and never let me catch you fishing in this childish and greedy manner again.'

'Come, come,' said the kind Admiral. 'The lad would have preferred the river, no doubt, but since you had forbidden it, what could he do? Sport is sport.'

'It's far more difficult than real fishing,' said George.

'Nonsense, sir, nonsense,' said his father. 'A baby could hook things off a tray passing underneath.'

'Could he, just! You try!' said George indignantly. 'Here is Golightly coming again. Just you get one of those sponge-cakes.'

Mr Chubb seized the rod and dangled the hook all ready, and as Golightly passed underneath he endeavoured to whisk it into the dish of sponge-cakes; but the hook unfortunately caught the handle of the tea-pot with a jerk instead. Over went the tea-pot at once, the boiling tea was upset. Golightly dropped the tray, and began to hop about, holding his right leg and roaring with pain.

Poor Mr Chubb, full of remorse, ran downstairs, rod in hand, to Golightly's assistance, but happening to tread on the butter dish, it slid from under his feet, so that he fell across the drawing-room doorway just as the ladies rushed out to see what could be the matter.

Aunt Emily, who was the first to appear, of course tripped over him, but the Duchess, who was gifted with great presence of mind, saved herself by clutching at the door-post, and, being accustomed to take the lead, rose at once to the situation.

'Let everyone be silent except the sufferers!' she cried, in a tone of command which instantly hushed all but Golightly, who continued to hop round, and was now calling wildly for brandy. 'Now, who is hurt, and where? I am well accustomed to rendering first aid. Let this poor man be carried at once into the drawing-room and laid upon the writing-table.'

The butler and footman, who had hastened to the hall on hearing the commotion, took Golightly by the head and the heels, and laid him, as her Grace directed, upon the writing-table; and very uncomfortable he found it, as they omitted to remove the ormolu and turquoise blotting-book and pen-tray before placing him there.

The Duchess then sent everyone flying in various directions at once for bandages, oil, and cotton wool, while she endeavoured in vain to hack through the tough leather of Golightly's boot with a penknife on one side, assisted by the Admiral's wife with a pair of scissors on the other.

Selfish Cissie and Greedy George, instead of concerning themselves with poor Golightly's sufferings, were busily picking the cakes out of the *débris* in the hall, and eating or pocketing them as fast as possible; but in the confusion this shocking behaviour passed unnoticed, except by Margery, who never could be taught to remember that she should remain in the still-room, and who now ran in with the kitchen dredger, dropping flour over the carpet on her way.

'But I don't see how the tea *could* have scalded his foot through that thick boot,' said sharp little Emily.

'No more it did, miss, but they won't listen to me,' said Golightly. 'Oh—oh—oh!'

Here the Duchess unluckily cut a little too deep, and reached the foot at last; the penknife broke in her hand, and Golightly sprang off the table and fled with the blade sticking out of his boot, followed by Margery, who was determined to flour him well the moment she succeeded in catching him.

'Well – really – that he should bolt away like that – without even thanking you for your trouble, dear Duchess!' said the Admiral's wife indignantly. 'What are servants coming to?'

'This is rank ingratitude,' said the Duchess, hardly able to believe her own eyes, as Golightly vanished round the corner. 'Somebody ought to have held him down.'

The two Miss Pitts, who had been growing more offended every moment, now advanced to take leave.

'Please, please wait for tea,' said poor Mrs Chubb; 'I assure you it won't be long.'

'You will forgive us for mentioning it, I am sure,' said the elder Miss Pitt, who was the soul of courtesy, 'but my sister and I have been seated here already for nearly half an hour, and no one has yet spoken to us or taken the least notice of our very existence.'

'I am sure I beg your pardon, but, one way and another, I have been very much flurried this afternoon,' said poor Mrs Chubb, bursting into tears, 'and the fact is I entirely overlooked you, though with the best intentions, through not being much accustomed to afternoon callers.'

The Miss Pitts were very kind-hearted, and could not bear to see anyone cry; moreover, they reflected that if they stayed on they might yet be introduced to the Duchess, so they consented to remain.

Margery then came in with fresh tea, the footman with more cakes, and the Admiral with dry boots, so that they were all seated happily round the tea-table, when the door opened and little William appeared in his night-shirt.

'William! What do you mean by this behaviour?' said his father, almost fainting with horror.

'What have I done now?' said William resentfully. 'George said you particularly mentioned I was to come just as I was, and that your motto was prompt obedience.'

'Come, come, Mr Chubb, I heard the message,' said the Admiral. 'Georgiana, love, have you half-a-crown about you?'

'No, Admiral, I haven't, and if I had I shouldn't permit you to squander it in tips,' said his wife severely.

'William, go to bed,' said Mr Chubb.

'Pray, pray don't send him away. He looks like a cherub,' cried the two Miss Pitts.

'Mr Chubb, you are unreasonable,' said the Duchess. 'I insist upon William's remaining where he is. If you are afraid of his taking cold, he can wear my feather boa,' and before William could resist he found himself sitting in the lap of the Duchess and being fed with strawberries and cream.

Meantime Charles had gone some way into the woods without finding anything to shoot; he now, taught by experience, moved as cautiously as possible, and presently his patience was rewarded, for he observed a rabbit sitting motionless at the foot of a hollow tree, and crept closer and closer until he felt quite certain that it would be next to impossible to miss it.

With beating heart he then took a careful aim, and fired.

There was a loud and piercing scream, the rabbit was scattered in every direction at once, and a man's head popped suddenly out of the tree and back again like a jack-in-the box.

Charles was so startled that he almost dropped the gun, and as he was always angry when he was frightened, he called out, 'What are you doing in that tree?' as loudly as he could.

'I refuse to answer until you have put down that murderous weapon,' said a shaking voice.

'I can't have hit him,' thought Charles, greatly relieved, 'or he would have mentioned it. It's not loaded,' he said aloud.

'Loaded or unloaded, a gun is a gun,' said the voice from the inner recesses of the tree. 'I shall not stir until I see you put it down.'

'Well, I've put it down. Now come out. You're trespassing, you know,' said Charles, beginning to recover his own courage. 'I suppose you're a poacher.'

'I'm nothing of the sort. My name is Higginbotham, and being much interested in natural history, I am trying to find a squirrel's nest in this tree,' said the voice indignantly.

'Why! You're the new tutor,' said Charles, feeling rather uncomfortable; 'I'm one of your pupils, Charles Chubb.'

'Then all I can say is that we have made a most unfortunate beginning, Charles,' said Mr Higginbotham, and he squeezed himself out of the tree and looked reproachfully at Charles.

'I call it a very fortunate one,' said Charles. 'If you'd looked out a moment sooner, I might have shot you – of course it would have been an accident,' he added hastily.

'I can hardly think it would have been an accident, Charles,' said Mr Higginbotham resentfully, 'for you deliberately aimed your gun at the tree.'

'How could I tell you were in the tree? I aimed at the rabbit.'

'At my rabbit!' cried Mr Higginbotham, in agonised tones. 'And did you hit it? Where is it?'

'I didn't know it was *your* rabbit; all I saw was a rabbit sitting under the tree with its tail cocked up all ready to be shot.'

'What have you done? It's not a live rabbit,' said Mr Higginbotham.

'It certainly isn't,' said Charles. 'I must have come too close to it, for I blew it all to bits.'

'It was filled with chocolates to the very brim,' said Mr Higginbotham, almost sobbing. 'Oh, what will my aunt say!'

'Of course, I'm very sorry if she was fond of it, though I didn't know rabbits liked chocolate,' said Charles, astonished; 'and I should think it would have died anyway, if it had eaten so much as all that.'

Mr Higginbotham took out his glasses, wiped them, and began to search at the foot of the tree.

'There may be a little chocolate left,' he said. 'I can't bear to think of it all being wasted. My aunt purchased that rabbit in the arcade, thinking it would be a pleasant surprise for my pupils.'

'Was it a sham rabbit, then?' said Charles, disgusted.

'It was a toy rabbit.'

'I suppose she thought we were mere kids,' said Charles. 'Even William would be too old to play with a thing like that.'

'Your father said you were all ages,' said Mr Higginbotham meekly.

'Oh, if she meant it for Teddy, of course it was very kind of her,' said Charles as gratefully as he could.

'Its body was hollow,' said Mr Higginbotham mournfully, 'and it was filled with . . .' He pounced joyfully on a chocolate cream. 'There! I hope you will gratify me by tasting it.'

Charles gratified him at once.

'I trust that we shall get on well together,' said Mr Higginbotham.

'I feel sure we shall,' said Charles thoughtfully, 'especially if you can get over your nervousness of firearms.'

'I have a naturally timid disposition, but I will do my best,' said Mr Higginbotham.

'My father would not like to know you were afraid of a gun, as he is anxious we should be good sportsmen,' said Charles.

'It can form no part of my duties to go out shooting, surely,' said Mr Higginbotham, alarmed. 'But I will certainly endeavour to conceal my terror as far as possible rather than annoy your dear father.'

'Then I advise you, if you'll excuse me, to go back to the house carrying the empty gun,' said Charles. 'I will take your Gladstone bag.'

'Be very careful, then, Charles, for the lock is not as secure as I could wish, and it contains my little all,' entreated Mr Higginbotham. 'I have carried it from the station to save a cab.'

'We could have sent to meet you, sir,' said Charles, for he had a kind heart. 'Your bag is pretty heavy.'

'Yes, but I did not wish to put your father to expense or trouble. I have been brought up very carefully, and this is the first time I ever left my aunt,' said Mr Higginbotham, bursting into tears.

Charles soothed him as well as he could, but he could not help reflecting that Mr Higginbotham was a very curious kind of tutor for his father to have chosen.

'I suppose he knows lots of Latin and Greek,' he thought to himself, 'and father decided that would make up for everything.'

Busy Matilda, carrying the twins, and followed by Clumsy Caroline, soon found a retired spot in the park where she could give her little brother and sister a sun-bath, so she laid them both on the air-cushion, and spread the clothes of one of them (who turned out to be Josephus) upon the bushes to dry.

The babies were very happy kicking on the air-cushion, and for some time Matilda and Caroline were very happy watching them, when the sound of a child crying was suddenly heard.

'I do believe it's Teddy,' said Matilda, listening.

'It comes from the river,' said Caroline. 'Can he have fallen in?'

'Molly was with him, and we should hear her screaming,' said Matilda. 'Leave it to me, Caroline; I will go and see what has happened. Don't touch the twins. Collect their clothes in case they should blow away, and wait for me,' and, carefully rolling the babies on to the moss, she seized the air-cushion and flew like an arrow from a bow towards the river.

Caroline collected the clothes, rolled them into a bundle, and put them behind a stone; but hearing a scream from Matilda, as well as fresh cries from Teddy, her prudence was overcome by curiosity and alarm, and she ran after her sister as fast as she could, down the green slopes of the park to the banks of the river.

Here she found Matilda issuing directions to Teddy, while she perceived her unfortunate little brother dangling by his jacket from the bough of a tree which overhung the very centre of the stream.

'How did he get there?' cried Caroline, astonished.

'He must have climbed up that fat easy trunk and crept along the bough to the very end, and then tumbled off; and luckily a twig caught his jacket. Keep still, Teddy,' screamed Matilda, 'or you will certainly break the twig and fall into the water. Don't struggle any more. Leave it all to me, and I will come and fetch you.'

Casting wildly round for assistance, Matilda caught sight of the family washing coming back from the village in a donkey-cart driven by a very deaf, cross, and disagreeable old man.

The intelligent child did not hesitate for an instant. She ran up the grass bank to the side of the road, and without wasting a moment over explanations, dragged the top hamper off the load which was piled on the little cart.

This was a large, square, solid basket, which had been carefully placed on the top of the others because it contained Mr Chubb's best white shirts, all newly starched and glazed.

What was the astonishment of the old washer-man when Matilda pounced upon this, deliberately emptied the contents into the road, snatched away the rope which bound the load together, and ran away with basket and cord as fast as she could and without a single word of apology.

The old man, being unable to run as fast as Matilda, very wisely made no attempt to follow her on his own legs. He picked up the shirts, crammed them into the cart as best he could, climbed back onto the seat, turned the donkey's head towards the river, and whipped him up into a gallop.

The donkey was not accustomed to be whipped, and far less accustomed to gallop, but having started downhill with a heavy load behind him, he could not stop himself, but went faster and faster till he arrived in the hollow where the river lay, when he stopped short with his four feet together, and the old man and the linen baskets all shot over his head into the middle of the path.

Meanwhile Matilda tied one end of the rope to the basket and the other to the tree, and then, floating the air-cushion upon the water, she popped the basket over it like an extinguisher. The flat boarded bottom of the basket thus formed a neat raft, upon which she cautiously balanced herself, after taking off her shoes and stockings and rolling up her skirt as though to paddle. She then pushed off from the shore with a long stick, and found herself just underneath Teddy, with the rope stretched to its fullest extent. Teddy still hung suspended by his jacket, though he had obediently ceased to struggle, and was now placidly sucking his thumb, in spite of the discomfort of his position.

Matilda called to Caroline to climb the tree, which was, as she said, a remarkably easy tree to climb, since the trunk was broad and covered with most convenient little knobs; she then ordered her sister to creep along the bough until she could stretch out her hand far enough to unhook Teddy.

'A touch will do it,' she screamed excitedly; 'and I am here all ready to catch him, or to fish him out of the water if by any chance I happen to miss him.'

Caroline did what she was told, and she had hardly touched the bough from which Teddy was suspended before he fell off.

Fortunately he had but little way to fall, and still more fortunately he fell plump into Matilda's arms, and she was so glad to get him that she did not mind the bump in the least.

'Now we will go home together, Teddy,' she said soothingly, and Teddy laughed with delight. 'It is a little wet and uncomfortable, but you can hold on tightly to my waist, and I have only to pull myself along by the rope and we shall be on dry land in a moment.'

But here she reckoned without the old washer-man, who, having picked himself up in a somewhat dazed condition, and looked around, suddenly perceived his basket afloat on the river, with, as he thought, the naughty child who had stolen it using it as a raft to amuse herself and her little brother at his expense. It was enough to annoy even a kind old man, and the laundry-man was rather disagreeable than otherwise, so he determined to give Matilda a good fright, though he knew there was really no danger, since the river was so shallow that if she had but known it she could have walked ashore quite easily.

'Drat your impudence, making yourself fast to the tree with my own rope under my very nose!' he shouted. 'I'll learn you to steal my baskets and trample my nice clean clothes in the mud. Since you're so fond of boating, you can go on a voyage and try how you like it,' and he untied the cord and threw it into the river.

The basket immediately whirled round and round, and floated away on the current with poor Matilda and little Ted, who were out of sight before Caroline could get down from the tree; which she was afraid to do until the old man had packed his load into the cart once more and driven away with the washing, grumbling to himself. She then ran along the river bank as fast as she could, and being a very heedless child, she presently tripped over something and fell. As she picked herself up she perceived that the obstacle in her path was Molly, the maid, who was sleeping soundly, with her head on a convenient cushion of moss.

Caroline knew by experience how difficult it was to wake Molly, so she shook her violently, and was relieved to find that Molly opened one eye.

'Oh my! I've been asleep. Where's Master Ted?' she gasped, looking round.

'Well may you ask,' said Caroline. 'Come at once; I can't stop. He's in the middle of the river with Matilda, and I can't believe the basket will go on floating.'

She ran on without waiting to explain any further.

'What will Nanny say?' cried Molly, stumbling up half asleep. 'Oh dear, oh dear; I shall be sent away, I know I shall,' and she ran after Caroline as fast as she could.

Before they had gone far they met Charles and Mr Higginbotham, and the two joined in the chase without knowing why, except that Caroline waved her arms at them and pointed wildly to the river; and they almost knocked down Dorothea and the Mayor, who were strolling quietly towards them, but who now turned and hurried after them in great alarm.

Charles, being young and active, easily outstripped the others, and came up with the raft just as its progress was impeded by a large rock.

'Hold on, hold on to the rock!' cried Charles. 'It's quite shallow here. I'll wade out and get hold of your rope,' and he threw off his jacket and plunged into the water.

Poor Mr Higginbotham, arriving breathless, saw him in the water, but was too short-sighted to see the basket and its passengers, and concluded that Charles had lost his senses or fallen into the river; so, though he could not swim, he immediately jumped in after his pupil, holding the gun with one hand and clutching a bush with the other, and screaming for help at the top of his voice. The Mayor, Dorothea, Caroline, and Molly all clung to each other firmly on the bank; and the Mayor, who was nearest the water, stretched out a hand to Charles, who succeeded in catching the end of the rope and in pulling the basket to shore, where Matilda and Teddy were safely landed.

Mr Higginbotham, wet to the skin, was next assisted out of the water, and the Mayor advised him to run home as quickly as he could.

'But my Gladstone bag,' sobbed Mr Higginbotham. 'Charles, what have you done with my bag?'

'I dropped it,' said Charles. 'Never mind your bag now. Let's get home and change.'

'How can I change without it? I told you my little all was in my bag,' said Mr Higginbotham reproachfully. 'I insist upon its being found.'

He cried so bitterly that they felt obliged to pacify him, and presently the Gladstone bag was picked up, though the contents were all tumbled out onto the path.

'Leave it to me,' said Matilda, actively stuffing them in again, 'and don't lose a moment; you will both catch your deaths of cold.' And to encourage Mr Higginbotham to run, Charles took one of his hands and she took the other, and they raced him along until he was ready to drop, and begged for a moment to breathe.

'What's that little white parcel?' said Charles, stopping to examine it.

'It must have fallen out of my bag,' said Mr Higginbotham. 'I'm sure it's my little nightshirt; I remember it was rolled round my bottle of tooth-powder just like that.'

'It's the twins' clothes,' said Caroline. 'Oh, Matilda, we have forgotten all about them.'

'One can't think of everything,' said Matilda, annoyed. 'But they will be all right. We left them not far from here.'

'We left them *here*,' said Caroline, beginning to cry. 'I sat on that very stone.'

'We can't have left them here, or they would be here still,' argued Matilda. 'They can't walk.'

'Some tramp may have stolen them. There is a right of way on this road,' said Dorothea, opening her brown eyes in horror. 'The children of the wealthy are frequently kidnapped, and, for aught we know to the contrary, this country may be infested with brigands.'

'It is nothing of the kind,' said the Mayor, offended. 'Let me tell you, young lady, that a more respectable neighbourhood never existed. Crime is unknown in this parish – and, talking of crime, there is the policeman, who lives in the village at your very door, and complains of having nothing to do from morning till night. I should not be surprised if the honest fellow had already found the missing babes and taken them into safe custody.'

The policeman was standing by the side of the linen-cart, writing in his pocket-book, and the old laundry-man was holding him by a button of his uniform, talking to him eagerly.

When he saw Matilda he dropped the policeman's button immediately and flew at her, shrieking, 'Here she is, here she is, policeman. I give her in charge. She stole my linen-basket, and took her little brother for a ride on the river in it, thinking to make game of me. Ask her where it is now. Ask her what she has to say.'

'I have a great deal to say,' began Matilda, 'but . . .'

'Whatever you say will be used against you,' interrupted the policeman; 'just remember that,' and to Matilda's terror he wetted his thumb, turned over a page, and began writing again, after eyeing her severely.

'Officer, do not let your zeal outrun your discretion; I am here to answer for these young ladies,' said the Mayor pompously; and Dorothea, comparing this diminutive champion with the policeman who towered over him, could not help feeling that Sir Jeremy must really be a true knight in his heart after all.

'Lord! Sir Jeremy, what a turn you gave me! I didn't know you was here, your worship,' said the policeman, and his knees knocked together.

'The matter of the basket can be explained another time,' said the Mayor, waving his hand. 'No doubt compensation will be offered.'

'What's he saying?' said the old man angrily.

'He says, go 'ome and don't kick up any more noise, or you'll be committed for contempt!' shouted the policeman. 'And you will be paid for your basket, which is more than you deserve, you old poacher, you. *I* knows you!'

The laundry-man grumbled to himself inaudibly and drove away; and very glad Matilda and Caroline were to see him depart.

'We have now a case of kidnapping to consider against, officer,' said the Mayor. 'Two of the infant children of Mr Chubb of Finch Hall have strayed away.'

'They can't have *strayed*,' said Matilda.

'They may have *rolled*,' sobbed Caroline.

The policeman turned over a new page and wrote down Mr Chubb's address.

'A thorough search should be instituted,' said the Mayor. 'All those who are dry should now join the hunt. The others should continue their progress to the house.'

'I'm nearly dry,' said Charles, 'and in this weather it can't matter much if I'm not.'

'Charles, I know I shall take cold if I don't change every rag I have on,' said Mr Higginbotham unhappily; 'and I promised my aunt not to get my feet wet.'

'Then you had better run home by yourself, and take the gun and the Gladstone bag with you,' said Charles, 'and tell them what's happened. They may be growing anxious.'

'But if I *order* you to come with me,' said Mr Higginbotham, with chattering teeth.

'Nonsense, sir, nonsense!' said Sir Jeremy warmly. 'This young gentleman's first duty is to his little brother and sister, however young they may be. Besides, I can't have other people giving orders in my presence. You are merely hindering the search, and as Mayor of Burridge I insist on your running all the way to Finch Hall without a moment's delay.'

Mr Higginbotham was so much alarmed by the loudness of the Mayor's voice, and the threatening looks of the policeman, that he set off at once, forgetting that he did not even know the way, and unconscious that the clasp of his little bag had given way once more, and that the contents were dropping out one by one as he ran.

4

KIDNAPPING

The Duke of Pontypool always made a point of being extremely civil to his neighbours, but he was not fond of driving, so when the Duchess set out to call on Mr and Mrs Chubb, he said it would be a good opportunity for him to take a long walk, and that he would therefore follow her on foot.

The day was warm, and the Duke was both hot and tired by the time he entered the gates of the park; so that, although he was a very dignified man, he determined to rest himself for a moment

by the road-side and mop his brow; but since he felt it would not
do for him to be seen thus engaged, he picked his way carefully
into a retired hollow and there sank down upon the turf.

Scarcely was he seated when he heard a faint gurgling sound,
and without any further warning Josephus – who had been nearest
the edge of the mossy slope whereon the babies had been laid
by their elder sister – rolled suddenly down the bank and into the
daisies and buttercups at the Duke's feet; and there he lay blinking at the sky exactly as he had blinked at the Admiral in the
fountain.

The Duke was naturally startled, and being unaccustomed to
babies (for he had no children of his own), he did not know what
to do; but he was not to be frightened out of his native courtesy,
so he asked Josephus whether he had hurt himself, as politely
as possible.

Josephus, being only eleven weeks old, of course made no reply
to this inquiry, but he had a momentary spasm which the Duke
mistook for a smile, and his questioner therefore came to the conclusion that his sudden descent had left him uninjured.

'I suppose he is too young to speak,' said the Duke. 'This is a
very sad case. Evidently he has been decoyed to this secluded
spot, robbed of his clothes, and deserted. But his being unable
to talk will complicate matters very much. In common humanity
I must do what I can for him. I can't leave him here. Yet it will
look extremely odd if I arrive to pay an afternoon call with a baby
in my arms. In my position it is really not to be thought of. I
wonder if he can walk?'

The Duke picked up Josephus very gingerly, and gently sup-
porting him with one hand, endeavoured to place his feet on the
ground with the other.

Josephus immediately had another spasm; his head rolled from
side to side, and his knees doubled up underneath him.

'He can't even stand,' thought the Duke, much distressed.
'What can I do? I shall have to carry him, and he is so slippery
I would as soon, or far sooner, carry a live fish. I must wrap
him up in something.'

So he laid Josephus on the turf, and rolled him up as neatly as
he could in his silk pocket-handkerchief, tying it in a knot round
his middle.

'After all, he looks almost like a parcel. I dare say even if I meet anyone, they won't notice that there is a head sticking out at one end and two feet at the other. The little creature appears to have a peculiarly placid disposition, that is one comfort. I couldn't possibly attempt to carry him at all if he began to wriggle.'

In fact, only the Duke's extreme kindness of heart (which was generally concealed from the world by a fiery manner) could possibly have made him carry a parcel of any kind, such was his care for his personal dignity.

Hoping earnestly that he would meet no one who knew him, he now hooked his finger into the middle knot of his live bundle, and began to walk cautiously onwards towards his destination.

But he had only proceeded a few yards, when, to his great dismay, he perceived Jane, lying on her back in the moss, and playing with her toes.

For a moment he thought he must have inadvertently allowed Josephus to slip from the handkerchief; but no, there were his two little feet peeping out of the bundle he carried. It was evidently another baby.

'This is positively disgraceful,' said the Duke, beginning to lose his temper. 'In the whole course of my existence I never knew such a thing. I shall speak seriously to this Mr Chubb. Babies ought not to be scattered all over his park like mushrooms. In old Finch's time nothing of the kind would have been permitted. To mark my displeasure I shall leave this one to take care of itself.'

He looked defiantly at Jane and walked away. But he then perceived a herd of cattle slowly making its way to the river to drink, and at the same moment a piteous cry from Jane recalled him.

'I can't leave her to be trampled to death,' thought the poor Duke. 'She actually seems sensible of her danger, by the faces she is making at me. For Heaven's sake, child, don't scream like this; you quite unnerve me. I never could bear to see a lady in distress. What can I do? I haven't another pocket-handkerchief, and she is most insufficiently clad.'

He put down Josephus and fumbled in his pockets. At length he drew out an enormous envelope full of legal documents, which had that morning been sent him by his lawyer. These he emptied into another pocket, and with great care he inserted Jane into the empty envelope. With a little management he got her safely in up to the neck, and she fitted exactly. He put the envelope back into his pocket, so that nothing was to be seen of Jane but her little bald head. Finding herself warm and comfortable, she immediately fell asleep, and the Duke, congratulating himself upon his ingenuity, picked up Josephus again and hurried on to the Hall.

To his great joy, the first person he encountered upon arrival was his own footman, John, who had slipped round to the back premises to refresh himself with a glass of ale, and who was now returning to his post by the front door.

'Hi!' shouted the Duke. 'Come here.'

'Yes, your Grace,' said John, and he walked with dignity to meet the Duke.

'Take this parcel,' said the Duke.

John started back.

'It's a baby, your Grace.'

'I'm well aware of that. Do you suppose I don't know a baby when I see one?' said the Duke angrily. 'I've got another somewhere about me,' and he pulled out Jane in her envelope, and handed her carefully to John.

'Take these down to the village constable, and give them in charge,' said the Duke. 'I found them loitering suspiciously on the highway, with no visible means of support.'

'Yes, your Grace,' said John, trembling; 'but the Duchess . . .'

'Don't stop and argue,' said the Duke.

'But her Grace . . .' faltered John.

The Duke turned purple with fury, and John, who was terrified of his master, waited no more, but turned and ran down the drive as fast as he could, with the powder flying in clouds from his hair and his golden livery and silk stockings sparkling in the sun.

'I am sure I don't know what the Duchess will say' – he thought as he ran, with a twin in either hand – 'when she orders the carriage and finds me missing. The quicker I get back the better. No, no; I'm not going to stop for nobody.'

This was because he saw Matilda waving and making him frantic signs in the distance, but faithful John only shook his head and ran the faster.

Matilda pointed him out to the policeman, and the policeman

took a short cut, hid behind a bush, and pounced out upon John as he passed.

'Now then!' he cried, seizing him by the collar. 'I take you into custody for attempting to kidnap these here children.'

'But I was bringing them to you!' gasped John.

'A very likely story,' said the policeman. 'Why, you was running away from me to your hardest. Here is the thief, your worship, caught in the act.'

'Thief – nonsense! This is a most respectable man,' panted the Mayor, as soon as he was near enough to recognise John. 'One of the Duke of Pontypool's servants. He often opens the door of the castle to me. How are you, John?'

'I'm nicely, thank you, Sir Jeremy,' said John. 'But her Grace is waiting for me.'

'On no account keep the Duchess waiting,' said the Mayor, 'I will be answerable to the police.'

'Thank you, Sir Jeremy,' said John, and he was off like the wind.

'I shall be back again before the Duchess knows I'm gone, after all,' he thought, with great satisfaction.

On his way he found Mr Higginbotham wandering disconsolately along and crying. John had a kind heart, so he couldn't help stopping to ask him what was the matter.

'I've been carrying my little bag upside down without noticing it,' sobbed Mr Higginbotham, 'and most of the contents seem to have dropped out.'

'I thought I saw an old hair-brush on the road,' said John, 'but I was too much hurried to pick it up. Well, sir, you'd better go back and look for your things.'

'But I lost my way, and I cannot retrace my footsteps for fear of losing it again,' said Mr Higginbotham, shivering.

'Bless me, you're wet through, and you seem to be ill, sir,' said John, observing how his teeth chattered in his head.

'I'm not ill yet, but I soon shall be,' said Mr Higginbotham dismally. 'I jumped into the river.'

John now felt sure that Mr Higginbotham was a lunatic, so he assumed a soothing manner, and helped him to strap up the almost empty bag.

'You shouldn't have done that, sir – you might have been drowned; and I'm afraid you've wet your beautiful gun.' ('And a good thing too, or by the way he's carrying it he'd be shooting the first person he met,' thought John.)

'I'm a stranger here,' said Mr Higginbotham, and he laid his head against John's shoulder-knots, to John's great disgust, and wept more bitterly than ever. 'A stranger and an orphan. I suppose you are a servant of Mr Chubb's. Tell me your name. I seem to have taken a fancy to you.'

'I am in the service of the Duke and Duchess of Pontypool,' said John stiffly. 'My name is John, and we happen to be calling on the Chubbs. And that reminds me I can't stay chattering here, sir, for her Grace may be waiting for me.'

'Oh, John, don't leave me!' said Mr Higginbotham, clinging to his arm. 'I am only just beginning to feel at home with you, and I'm so cold.'

'Then the sooner you get to the house and have a drop of brandy, the better,' said John, and he picked up the gun and the bag and began running again, with Mr Higginbotham still clinging to his arm.

Golightly, who had recovered from his scald, and who was so jealous of his master's new servants that he took every opportunity of answering the bell himself, opened the front door to them; and John handed over the gun and bag to Mr Higginbotham, learnt that the ducal carriage had been asked for, and went off to the stables to get it, without a moment's delay.

'Blesh me!' said Golightly, who was still too much confused with the various remedies he had taken during the afternoon to notice Mr Higginbotham's piteous condition. 'What, another vishitor! What name shall I shay?'

'Mr Higginbotham. But I'm hardly in a fit state to see anyone at present. I should like to rest and change my clothes,' faltered poor Mr Higginbotham.

But it was too late, for the moment he uttered his name Golightly threw open the door and announced him.

He stood dripping on the threshold, looking round him with a deprecating smile, holding his bag in one hand and his gun, which was pointed straight at the tea-table, in the other.

The ladies all rose in alarm.

'Put that gun down at once, sir, whoever you are!' shouted the Duke, who was eating a muffin in the line of fire.

'We've had accidents enough for one afternoon,' said the Admiral, knocking up the muzzle of the gun with great presence of mind; then taking it away from the unresisting intruder, he put it carefully in a corner.

'I know that,' said Mr Higginbotham resentfully; 'I've had some very narrow escapes myself. I jumped into the river after my new pupil, Charles Chubb.'

'Charles!' screamed poor Mrs Chubb. 'Heaven bless you, Mr Higginbotham! You saved him?'

'No,' said Mr Higginbotham.

Mrs Chubb uttered a piercing scream and fell into Aunt Emily's arms.

'How could I save him? I can't even swim,' said Mr Higginbotham. 'I *knew* when I jumped in that I couldn't save anybody, but I deemed it my duty to try.'

'Don't stand there prating about yourself,' said Mr Chubb, much agitated. 'Tell us how Charles fell into the river. Speak, man, speak.'

'I never can speak when I'm flurried to this extent,' said Mr Higginbotham tearfully. 'Charles did not fall into the river at all. He jumped.'

'Why jumped?' said Aunt Emily, trembling.

'He saw his sister and his little brother in the middle of the stream,' began Mr Higginbotham.

Mrs Chubb screamed yet more loudly.

'Calm yourself, madam,' said the Admiral soothingly. 'The river running through your grounds is nowhere more than three feet deep.'

'But some of my children are not nearly three feet high,' sobbed Mrs Chubb.

'Once for all,' shouted the Duke, seizing Mr Higginbotham by the shoulder and shaking him soundly, 'will you or will you not have the goodness to tell this unfortunate lady how many of her family, roughly speaking, on the average, have been drowned? We don't ask for details.'

'Don't be so violent,' said Mr Higginbotham reproachfully. 'Nobody has been drowned. They are all coming home together, laughing and talking. I was just going to tell you so. Nobody has been hurt except me. I *might* have been drowned.'

'And why weren't you?' said the Duke angrily.

'The Mayor pulled me out,' said Mr Higginbotham, and he edged away from the Duke as far as possible, for fear of being shaken again.

'Very officious of him,' said the Duke, frowning. 'Sophia, this call has lasted long enough. Order the carriage.'

'I *have* ordered the carriage over and over again, but it doesn't come,' said the Duchess.

'Oh, ah; I remember now, I sent John on an errand,' said the Duke, rather confusedly.

'John. Is John *your* servant? I've taken *such* a fancy to him,' said Mr Higginbotham, beaming.

'I don't allow people to take fancies to my servants, sir!' thundered the Duke, who had taken a great dislike to Mr Higginbotham.

'William, take Mr Higginbotham upstairs and show him his room,' said Mr Chubb hastily. 'Golightly will get him everything he wants, and he must be tired after his journey.'

'Couldn't he be dried first? He will ruin the stair carpet,' said Mrs Chubb plaintively.

'Maria, will you never realise that stair carpets are now no object?' whispered Mr Chubb reprovingly.

'I have not your memory, Thomas,' said his wife meekly; 'and I am, besides, confused by so many visitors, and by hearing what sounds to me very like the twins crying in the hall.'

'We must be going,' said the Admiral hurriedly, for he felt he could not encounter the twins a second time.

'And there is our carriage at last,' said the Duchess, rising with great relief. 'Goodbye, Mrs Chubb. I hope you will allow some of your children to come and see me, and especially William.'

'Anything you like, I'm sure,' said poor Mrs Chubb, who was growing more tired of her visitors every moment. 'William, give the Duchess back her boa, and put on this antimacassar instead.'

William had had quite enough of sitting in the lap of the Duchess and being fed with sponge-cake dipped in tea (which she had been absently giving him at intervals, under the impression that he was too young to digest solid food), so he took the opportunity to escape, without availing himself of the offered wrap, calling to Mr Higginbotham to follow him upstairs.

'It must be delightful to have such a number of children,' said the elder Miss Pitt. 'Such a nice surprise for the neighbourhood, to find there are so many of you. I could sit here all day.'

'She *will*, if we don't take her away,' thought the Duchess; and she good-naturedly offered to give the two Miss Pitts a lift to the village, much to their delight and the disgust of the Duke, who was thus obliged to sit with his back to the horses, which never agreed with him.

'What did you do with the parcels, John?' said the Duke.

'I gave them to the constable, your Grace, but I've just seen them come back here again. They appear to belong to the house.'

'Drive home as fast as you can,' said the Duke in alarm.

'Well, Maria, I'm sure everything went off most successfully in the end, in spite of one or two little mishaps,' said Mr Chubb jovially.

'I'm glad you're pleased, Thomas, but as far as I was concerned, I have been sitting on thorns the whole afternoon. It's not so much what did happen, as what *might* have happened that it upsets me to think about,' said Mrs Chubb dismally.

'Nonsense, my love; you take a gloomy view,' said Mr Chubb.

'I see nothing for you to be upset about, Maria. All the children are safe and sound. I've just counted them,' said Aunt Emily. 'If you were bruised from head to foot as I am, through falling over Thomas when he was behaving in that extraordinary manner with a fishing-rod in the hall, you *might* have something to grumble at, I allow; it was most vexatious for me, practically turning a somersault before a room full of people.'

'Nonsense, Emily, nonsense! You should not permit yourself to be put out by such trifles,' said Mr Chubb severely. 'Life is full of ups and downs in a large family, and you must expect to have your share like the rest of us.'

5

THE SECRET STAIRCASE

Dreamy Dorothea loved mystery, and was always seeking romance; what, then, was her delight, when one evening, while earnestly gazing on a full-length portrait of a Cavalier ancestor, she perceived a white ivory button in the centre of a gilt rose upon the heavily ornamented frame. She was alone in the dim, oak-panelled dining-room, for she had just finished arranging the flowers on the dinner-table; and the candles were not yet lighted, as it wanted yet a quarter of an hour to her parents' dinner-time.

Glancing fearfully around her at the many other portraits upon the walls, she gently pressed the button, and, to her surprise and joy, the picture, frame and all, began to move. Very slowly it swung open, and she perceived that it formed a large door, whereof the hinges were concealed by the broad gilt edges of the frame. No sooner was it open than she saw before her a recess in the wall and a narrow staircase winding downwards.

Overjoyed by her discovery, Dorothea was just about to step inside, when her brother William came into the room and uttered a cry of astonishment.

'Promise not to tell,' said Dorothea hastily. ' 'Tis I who have discovered the secret of this old house. I believe this staircase leads to some forgotten dungeon, William, where perchance a skeleton miser is still seated beside a heap of gold or a casket of priceless jewels.'

'Let me come with you,' said William joyfully. 'I'll fetch my sword.'

'No, no,' said Dorothea; ' 'tis my quest, not yours!'

'Oh, all right,' said William, offended. And he turned and marched towards the door. 'I'm sure I don't want to come; only I thought, if you *did* see skeletons and things, you might be glad of someone with you who wasn't afraid of them. I know what cowards girls are!'

'Stop a moment, William,' said Dorothea, for on second thoughts she decided the staircase did look rather dark and solitary. 'Suppose I let you come, you'll keep my secret?'

'Am I Cissie, to go telling?' said William indignantly.

'Then you *shall* come. Hush! Here are the servants. We can't go now,' said Dorothea, hastily closing the picture again. 'After dinner, William, instead of going to bed, meet me on this spot, and we will explore together. Till then – silence!'

Both children were so excited that it seemed to them as though their parents' meal would never end. They sat together on the drawing-room sofa, and Dorothea told her little brother at great length of the treasure she hoped to discover in the dungeons, and what she intended to do with it. William grew so much interested that he could hardly be torn away from her side even when they were presently summoned to dessert; and Dorothea could not altogether refrain from mentioning the subject uppermost in her mind.

'Is this a very old house, Papa?' she asked as unconcernedly as possible.

'Yes, my child,' said Mr Chubb. 'The middle portion of the building dates from the reign of Henry the Eighth.'

'Caroline, in what year did Henry the Eighth ascend the throne?' said Miss Jenkins, who never lost an opportunity of improving her pupils' minds, even at meals.

Caroline's jaw dropped in dismay, but sharp little Emily replied without a moment's hesitation, '1702.'

'Emily, I am delighted to see that you profit so well by your studies,' said Mr Chubb warmly. 'Caroline, I blush for you.'

Here Miss Jenkins had a severe fit of coughing.

'But it wasn't 1702,' said Wilful William.

'I never said it was, William,' said his father, with great dignity. 'Your little sister cannot at her age be expected to know everything. Her willing spirit makes amends for any trifling inaccuracy of detail . . .'

'She's one hundred and ninety-three years wrong,' said William.

'. . . and contrasts most favourably with Caroline's supineness and your own positive passion for setting your elders to rights,' ended Mr Chubb severely. 'Hold your tongue, sir, and finish your strawberries.'

Wilful William was about to reply, but Dorothea made him an agonised sign to be silent, and Emily squeezed his hand under the table, so he said no more.

As soon as dessert was over the younger children were sent to bed; Mr Chubb locked up the decanters in the sideboard, which he was always obliged to do on Golightly's account, and then he blew out the candles, rang for the servants to clear away, and followed Mrs Chubb and Aunt Emily to the drawing-room.

A few minutes later Dorothea crept softly back to the deserted dining-room, and there found William, with his sword-belt buckled about his waist and the lantern from Charles's photographic dark-room in his hand.

'Dear me, how clever of you to think of that. I forgot we should want a light,' said Dorothea, whose only preparation had been to place a rose in her dark hair, lest by any chance she should meet the ghost of the handsome Cavalier.

William held up the lantern, and she found and pressed once more the button in the frame.

The picture swung slowly open again, and disclosed the staircase.

'Don't let's quite shut it,' whispered Dorothea, as she stepped inside the recess and looked fearfully down into the darkness. 'If we pull it to that will be enough. We might not find it so easy to open from this side.'

They pulled it to behind them, and then began very cautiously to descend the staircase.

Meanwhile Mrs Chubb discovered that she had dropped her fan, her gloves, and her lace pocket-handkerchief under the dinner table, so she returned quietly to the dining-room to pick them up. The poor lady was of a very nervous temperament, and as she was not fond of the moonlight, which was now streaming through the uncurtained windows, she took a candlestick from the hall table to light her on her way. But as she entered she was startled to perceive the picture of the Cavalier suddenly leave the wall where it had always hung, advance, as it seemed, into the middle of the room to meet her, and then slowly return to its usual position.

She uttered a loud scream, and remained rooted to the spot, with the candle in her hand, too much terrified to move, and Mr Chubb and Aunt Emily flew to her assistance.

'What are you doing in here, Maria?' said Mr Chubb, astonished.

'I came for my fan and gloves,' said Mrs Chubb faintly, 'and if you will believe me, Thomas, the Cavalier deliberately came off the wall to meet me. I assure you I am trembling in every limb.'

'I certainly do not believe you, Maria,' said Mr Chubb warmly. 'This is what comes of eating Welsh rabbit. I told you how unwholesome it was. Your digestion is disordered, and your imagination consequently has played you this trick.'

'I am fond of toasted cheese, Thomas; it is so long since we had anything so nice and homely,' said Mrs Chubb humbly. 'Somehow I seemed to fancy it.'

'Just so, and now you seem to fancy the Cavalier is moving,' said Mr Chubb triumphantly. 'One fancy leads to another, as a matter of course. Bless me, what's that?'

It was Aunt Emily's turn to scream.

'I saw a crack of light behind the picture, Thomas, believe me or not as you choose,' she said.

'Nonsense!' said Mr Chubb, but he turned pale.

At this moment the draught of the open door and window

appeared to affect the Cavalier's portrait strangely. It quivered unmistakably, and once more swung slowly outwards and stood in the middle of the room as Mrs Chubb had described.

'This is a most extraordinary thing,' said Mr Chubb, in a whisper. 'Don't be frightened, Maria. Give me your hand, and I will go and see what it means.'

'You shall not go alone,' said Aunt Emily heroically, and she clung to her sister's other arm. They all advanced towards the picture firmly, and, after a moment's hesitation, walked past it, and found the open doorway and staircase behind.

'The picture is a door,' said Mr Chubb. 'How very absurd, my dear Maria, that it should have alarmed you so terribly. This is evidently a priest's hiding place of the olden time. I shall go down and see where it leads to.'

'Thomas, you shall not. I cannot allow you to risk your life. Think of your eleven children,' said Mrs Chubb.

'I do think of them, and in their interests I must know the ins and outs of our new home,' said Mr Chubb. 'It may be there is a chamber of hidden treasure below.'

'What do we want with hidden treasure? We are already too rich,' said Mrs Chubb, wringing her hands.

'Speak for yourself, Maria,' said Aunt Emily. '*I* am not too rich; and if we do discover treasure, I shall insist upon getting my share. I am going with you, Thomas.'

'Very well,' said Mr Chubb, 'you shall do as you choose, Emily,' and he stepped onto the staircase, followed closely by Aunt Emily.

'Wait for me, I implore you! I cannot be left behind,' shrieked Mrs Chubb in terror; and she hurried in after them, just as the picture swung back to the wall once more, but this time it closed with a sharp click, and the slight draught that ensued suddenly blew out the candles, which Mr Chubb had taken from his wife and Aunt Emily and was holding aloft.

'This is very awkward indeed,' said Mr Chubb, who had already descended several steps. 'We must go back and get a light.'

'It is all very well to say go back, Thomas,' said Aunt Emily, 'but I am afraid to go either backwards or forwards in the dark. The stairs are very narrow, and I am practically wedged between the two walls.'

'I cannot find any handle or lock or key or opening of any kind,' said Mrs Chubb, groping about with her hands where she had imagined the door to be. 'I can feel nothing at all but cobwebs.'

'Odd. I keep fancying I see a gleam of red light on the wall just below me. Can the place be on fire?' said Mr Chubb nervously.

At this moment a loud sneeze startled them all, and Mrs Chubb screamed again.

'It's only me,' said Dorothea's voice meekly. 'Don't be frightened, Mamma.'

'Dorothea, what are you doing here?' said her father sternly.

'*I* discovered this place,' said Dorothea, 'and I brought William with me to explore, and we heard voices just above us, so we came softly back to see who it was.'

'William,' said Mr Chubb, 'did I or did I not send you to bed?'

'It was my fault,' said Dorothea, 'and I don't know what we should do without him, for he has brought Charles's dark lantern with him.'

William now produced the lantern, which he had been holding behind him, and uncovered the dark slide. They perceived that they were all standing one above the other, on a spiral staircase, with rough masonry on either side of them.

'As I have got the light,' said William, starting off as quickly as he could, for fear his father should take it away from him, 'I'd best go on in front.'

'Do not go too fast, or you will break your neck,' said Mr Chubb; but William went as fast as he could, and they all filed after him till they came to the bottom of the steps. Here was another door, which for some time they could not open; but Dorothea, guessing that there must be the same kind of concealed spring here as in the picture, sought for and found the button, pressed it, and the heavy, iron-studded door slowly opened. They all entered a low, vaulted hall, and the door shut behind them with a loud resounding clang that echoed through the vaults. However, they were by this time too much excited to be alarmed, and pressed eagerly forward to examine the apartment by the light of William's lantern.

It was empty, but on every side low stone archways tempted them to explore a little further.

'Let us keep together,' said Mr Chubb. 'You can all follow me.

These are the vaults over which the original house was built, and I believe these are Norman pillars.'

'You don't say so, Thomas!' said Aunt Emily in awestruck tones.

'It is very cold and damp, Thomas, Norman pillars or no Norman pillars,' said Mrs Chubb, shivering; 'and I can't see a sign of the treasures you were talking about,' she added, when they had wandered in and out of the archways for some time, always finding themselves back again eventually in the vaulted chamber.

'Do not be too sure, Maria,' cried Mr Chubb excitedly. 'What is this? I find one of these archways in the wall has been artfully filled up with planks and whitened to resemble stone. Listen! It is quite hollow.'

'Can it be another door?' suggested Dorothea.

'No, no, it is a partition,' said Aunt Emily; 'but I cannot see any means of opening it.'

Mr Chubb, however, was not to be overcome by trifles.

'The partition appears to me to be quite a flimsy one,' he said. 'Emily, you are the heaviest of the party . . .'

'I cannot allow, Thomas, that I am any heavier than you are,' said Aunt Emily, offended.

'Is this a moment to dispute over our respective weights, Emily?' asked Mr Chubb mildly. 'Surely it is rather an opportunity to unite them in forcing down this obstacle in our path. Place your shoulder here, and when I say *three*, push with all your might. Now then. One, two, three!'

At the word *three*, Mr Chubb and Aunt Emily hurled themselves against the partition with such force that it gave way, and Aunt Emily fell through to the other side.

There was a faint scream, the crash of breaking bottles, and a strong smell of sherry.

'We must have got into the wine-cellar,' said Mr Chubb, much disconcerted. 'I hope you are not hurt, Emily?'

'I am very much hurt indeed, Thomas,' said poor Aunt Emily, weeping.

William and Dorothea assisted their father to tear down the remaining boards of the partition, and held up the lantern, when Aunt Emily was discovered to be sitting on a heap of broken bottles, with wine streaming over the floor beneath her in every direction.

'I can't think why I am not cut to pieces with all this broken glass about,' sobbed Aunt Emily.

'You must be thankful you have on the thick velvet dress lined with silk which I gave you the other day, Emily,' said Mr Chubb. 'That alone could have saved you from serious injury.'

'How can I be thankful that my best dress is soaked through and through with sherry, and ruined for ever, Thomas?' said Aunt Emily peevishly. 'You ask impossibilities.'

'I wonder what sherry it is? Can it be – I'm afraid . . . Yes, it *is* poor cousin Joseph's best old brown sherry with the yellow seal,' cried Mr Chubb, in a voice of agony. 'I remember it was exactly opposite the champagne.'

'What can it matter what sherry it is, so long as dear Emily is safe?' said Mrs Chubb. 'Do, pray, Thomas, now that you know where we are, let us get upstairs immediately before any more accidents happen.'

'Of course I know where we are. It is obvious to the meanest capacity that it must be the wine-cellar, since poor Emily (though I am far from blaming her) fell into the sherry bin,' said Mr Chubb; 'but I cannot believe that the secret staircase was merely a short cut from the dining-room to the wine-cellar. And I shall continue to explore until I am quite certain. You can go back as soon as you choose, Maria.'

'But *how* can I go back, Thomas?' said Mrs Chubb. 'I am sure I am only too willing to return, for I am half dead with sleep.'

'I can let you out through the cellar door,' said Mr Chubb, feeling in his pocket. 'No, I can't. Bless me, I forgot. The cellar key is locked up in my desk. Well, you must go back the way you came.'

But in vain did William hold up his lantern, and Dorothea search for buttons. In vain did they all knock and kick and shout. In vain did Aunt Emily and Mr Chubb put their shoulders against the stout oaken door by which they had entered the vaulted chamber. It remained perfectly unmoved by all their efforts. Their calls for help echoed through the low archways, and no one came to their assistance.

'The household should all have retired by this time, if they have obeyed my orders,' said Mr Chubb, looking at his watch in the light of the lantern. 'It is past eleven o'clock. I am afraid, Maria,' he added, with a ghastly smile, 'that we may be obliged to remain here all night.'

'Hurrah!' said William, delighted.

'What a splendid adventure!' said Dorothea, clasping her hands.

'Children, be silent,' said Mr Chubb dejectedly. 'Emily, I beseech you not to cry.'

'How can I help crying?' retorted Aunt Emily. 'It is all very well to talk of stopping here all night, but, so far as I can see, we are much more likely to stop here for ever.'

'Perchance our mouldering skeletons may be found here fifty years hence,' said Dorothea ecstatically. 'When Charles is an old, old man, he will perhaps discover us, and understand for the first time the cause of our mysterious disappearance.'

'What rot!' said William. 'Is it likely that Charles would wait fifty years before coming to the cellar? Besides, he will be wanting the champagne for his coming of age.'

'William, once for all, be silent!' said his father. 'This is not a subject for joking.'

'I *wasn't* joking,' said William, indignantly. 'I was talking plain common sense.'

'Thomas, if we wander round and round this place any longer I shall drop,' said Mrs Chubb. 'If there isn't any other kind of seat to be found, I must sit on the edge of a wine-bin. And I am sure it would warm us all if we drank a little of the sherry Emily has unintentionally opened for us.'

'We cannot drink out of broken glass, Maria.'

'I have a tin mug in my pocket,' said William, producing it, 'and some biscuits, if you feel hungry, Mamma.'

'I commend your forethought, William, though I deprecate the habit of carrying loose food in the pockets,' said Mr Chubb.

'It wasn't very likely I should take Dorothea exploring without any provisions,' said William.

Drinking sherry out of the tin mug, and eating the biscuits, occupied them all happily for a few moments, as they sat on the edge of a wine-bin, in a row; but a fresh misfortune now happened, for the small oil lamp in the lantern suddenly flickered and burned out before Mr Chubb could light the candle he held.

There they now had to sit motionless in the dark, for they were afraid of moving, with so much broken glass scattered all over the cellar floor.

'Do you think you could get a little nap, Maria?' said Mr Chubb, always thoughtful for his wife's comfort.

'No, Thomas, I should think it most unlikely. I find the stone very cold to sit upon, and my shoes are full of sherry,' said Mrs Chubb, as patiently as she could.

'I have an idea,' said Aunt Emily, with a suddenness that made them all jump.

'What is it?' said Mr Chubb eagerly.

'Suppose I sing to you,' said Aunt Emily. 'I have often heard that shipwrecked mariners keep up each other's spirits that way, and I know several of my songs by heart.'

'I am very sorry, Emily, but I must beg you to refrain from doing anything of the kind,' said Mr Chubb angrily. 'It would be the last straw. I am not fond of music at the best of times, as you know very well.'

'What are you doing, Dorothea?' said her mother, hearing a faint rustle of paper.

'I am scribbling a few thoughts on the occasion,' said the poetess modestly.

'What can you have to scribble about at a moment like this?' said her father.

'I am sure, Thomas, if the poor child can comfort herself by scribbling, there's no reason why we should prevent her,' said Mrs Chubb. 'Though how she can write in the dark I don't know.'

'I often do, when I am suddenly inspired in the night,' said Dorothea meekly. 'However, if I learn my lines by heart as soon as I compose them, that generally does very well till the morning.'

'It might comfort us all a bit if you recited them now,' said Aunt Emily. 'Unless your father objects.'

'Not at all,' said Mr Chubb. 'I do not dislike Dorothea's poetry. I fancy she inherited her facility from me. I used to compose excellent Latin verse in my youth.'

'I do not like reciting my own verses as a rule,' said Dorothea doubtfully; 'still – if they would comfort you . . .'

She repeated the following lines in a hollow voice which reverberated through the cellar:

Five puny mortals, three were passing old,
  Though two were young and fair,
Yet all athirst and ravenous for gold,
  Stole down the secret stair.

There in the bowels of the earth they groped
  For hidden hoards of yore;
Great glut of riches hungrily they hoped,
  Though they had boundless store.

Fate then advanced on them with outstretched shears,
And chopped their lives in twain:
Nor those of tough nor those of tender years
  Knew greed of gold again.

'I never remember to have heard myself described as a *puny mortal* before,' said Mr Chubb, after a short silence.

'I cannot think it dutiful of you, Dorothea, to call either your parents or myself *passing old* and *tough*,' said Aunt Emily resentfully. 'I don't see what comfort you could expect us to find in such epithets.'

'One cannot always say what one means in a poem, Aunt Emily,' said Dorothea gently. 'There are the rhymes to be considered.'

'I am sure it is very good; you can't expect her to make no mistakes at all at her age,' said Mrs Chubb indulgently.

'I could wish her poems were a little more cheerful, Maria; but she has inherited the melancholy Finch disposition, I fear,' said Mr Chubb, sighing.

'Papa,' said William, 'I heard a footstep.'

'Nonsense,' said Mr Chubb, but they all listened intently, with cold shivers running up and down their spines. 'Don't breathe so heavily, Emily,' whispered Mr Chubb.

'I *must* breathe, Thomas,' said Aunt Emily peevishly. 'Footsteps or no footsteps, I cannot asphyxiate myself to please you.'

'Be silent,' said Mr Chubb in agonised tones. 'There *is* a footstep.'

Sure enough a footstep was heard, followed by a slight clanking sound.

'It is a spectre, dragging its chains,' murmured Dorothea.

'Or a burglar,' suggested William hardly above his breath, and he unsheathed his little sword, determined to sell his life dearly, and really wondering if any boy had ever passed such a thoroughly enjoyable night before.

Mrs Chubb suppressed a scream with difficulty.

'Do not make a sound,' entreated Mr Chubb.

The footsteps drew closer, and a light gleamed unmistakably through the keyhole of the cellar door.

There was the sound of a key being slowly inserted in the lock.

Mr Chubb gathered himself together for a spring.

The key turned, the creaking door was pushed open, and the face of Golightly, illuminated by a kitchen candle, appeared in the doorway.

With a bound his master was upon him. The candle rolled to the ground and was extinguished, and Golightly, with a yell of terror, fell upon his knees.

'What are you doing here, sir?' said Mr Chubb, not relaxing his hold of Golightly's collar for a moment.

'I found a key as fitted – the duplicate of yours – directly we came. I've been a drinking of the old brown sherry regular when the fambly was gone to bed,' said Golightly, trembling; 'but I'll never do it again, sir, so long as I live.'

'I'll take care you don't,' said Mr Chubb, sternly. 'Have you got a match about you?'

'Yes, sir. There's a box of vestas in my weskit pocket,' sobbed Golightly.

'How often have I desired you to use nothing but safeties?' said Mr Chubb. 'Light the candle at once.'

The shaking Golightly lit the candle, and surveyed the procession, which now picked its way cautiously over the broken glass of the cellar, with an astonishment that bordered on insanity.

Mr Chubb locked the cellar door and put Golightly's duplicate key in his pocket, and the explorers all mounted the back stairs very thankfully and went to bed.

6

VISITING THE POOR

One day Meddling Matilda heard her mamma lamenting that she
was not strong enough to go out and visit her poorer neighbours
as often as she could wish, so she determined, without saying a
word to anyone, to relieve her parent of this duty by undertaking
it herself.

As she was not allowed to go out alone, she was,
however, obliged to take Clumsy Caroline into her confidence;
and the two slipped off together immediately after luncheon,
unobserved by their elders, and carrying a large covered
basket.

'What have you got there?' asked Caroline.

'You shouldn't ask questions, child,' said Matilda, who since

her arrival at Finch Hall often put on the airs of a grown-up
person, though she was but thirteen.

'If you won't tell me, I don't want to come at all,' said Caroline,
offended; 'and I shall tell Aunt Emily where you've gone. I know
she wouldn't like your going to visit the poor by yourself.'

'I consider that I am obeying my parents' wishes by going,'
said Matilda indignantly. 'Papa said I was to save Mamma all the
trouble I could, and Mamma said one should never go among the
poor empty-handed. As for Aunt Emily, she may *think* she knows
better than I do, but it is a matter of opinion.'

'Well, what have you got in the basket?'

'I have got some little comforts for the old and sick, and some
pretty things to decorate the home,' said Matilda importantly.
'You will see them as I unpack them. Now, where shall we go
first?'

'We had better begin at the top of the street and work downwards,' said Caroline.

Musbury was a very small village, with a single street, and just
now it looked somewhat deserted, for the men were away at work,
the children at school, and the women busy indoors.

'I think we will begin with the prettiest first,' said Matilda, and
they walked up a narrow pathway to a cottage covered with
Virginian creeper, and knocked rather nervously at the door.
Nobody answered.

After knocking for some time Matilda grew so impatient that
she lifted the latch and looked in.

There sat a very old man in an armchair by the fire (though it
was a hot summer afternoon), with his face turned towards them,
and on it a very cross expression indeed. The room was spotlessly
clean, and the tin kettle shone like silver.

'How very odd of him not to answer our knocking,' whispered
Matilda to Caroline, feeling rather offended at the rude manner
in which the old man glared at them without speaking.

'Perhaps he's deaf,' whispered Caroline.

The old man *was* very deaf, and he had not heard the knocking
on his door; but he saw Matilda and Caroline enter, and observed
quickly enough that they were whispering to each other.

'What do you want here?' he said in a snappish tone.

'We have come to see you,' said Matilda.

'What?' said the old man. 'Come inside and shut the door, can't you? I feel the draught something dreadful. Now put down your basket and speak up. I'm rather hard of hearing.'

'We've come to see you,' shouted Matilda.

'Come to what?' said the old man.

'I'll give him a present,' said Matilda to Caroline. 'Then he'll understand.'

So she smiled at the old man as winningly as she could.

'Don't you make faces at me,' he growled. 'Just tell me your business, and be done with it.'

Matilda ceased to smile, and stooped down to get something out of her basket.

'I don't want to buy nothing, if that's what you're after,' said the old man suspiciously.

'I'm not asking you to buy anything,' screamed Matilda, and she took a bottle triumphantly out of the basket and handed it to him.

'That'll soften him,' she said to Caroline. 'All old men like whisky; it's nearly half full. I got it off the dining-room sideboard. I knew it could be spared, for I heard Papa say there were several dozen bottles of it in the cellar.'

'What's this?' said the old man sternly.

He pulled the cork out, smelt it, and started back in horror.

'This here's intoxicating liquor,' he said indignantly. 'What are you young warmints doing trapesing about with whisky? Who put you up to this, I should like to know?'

'We thought you'd like to drink it,' shouted Matilda; but as she could not make him hear, she illustrated her meaning in vivid pantomime, pointing to the bottle, and pouring imaginary whisky into an imaginary tumbler and tossing it off.

'You bad little gal,' said the old man, shocked. 'Do you mean you can drink off spirits like that at your age?'

'No, no!' said Matilda in despair.

'Where's my ear-trumpet?' said the old man.

He got out of his chair and hobbled about in search of it. At last he discovered it quite close to Caroline's hand.

'Why didn't you tell me where it was?' he said crossly. 'Here it is all the time.'

'I didn't know this was that,' said poor Caroline, terrified by his scowl.

'Now then,' said the old man, and he sat down, still holding the bottle of whisky firmly by the neck. 'Speak into this trumpet and tell me what all this means, and what you two warmints have come here disturbing of me for.'

Matilda thought the old man was very disrespectful, and, glancing hastily at Caroline, could not help wishing they had put on their best frocks, instead of thoughtlessly rushing out in their stained overalls and oldest hats, all ready, as Nanny had supposed, for a romp in the garden, so that they looked much more like a pair of untidy school-children than the elegant young ladies she would have liked them to appear.

To atone for the deficiency, she assumed her most dignified manner, and putting her mouth close to the ear-trumpet, shouted as loudly as she could:

'We are from Finch Hall.'

Now, Matilda did not know that it is extremely painful to the deaf to be shouted at through an ear-trumpet, which of course magnifies sound enormously, so she was surprised when the old man jumped backwards and dropped the trumpet on to the floor.

'You bad gal!' he cried furiously. 'Haven't you got more sense than to bellow at me like that? Pick that thing up at once and see if it's broken.'

Matilda picked it up and handed it to him, trembling, and he examined it carefully, grumbling to himself all the time.

'If it had been broke, I'd have made you pay for it, mind that,' he said. 'Now what's your business? I can't be worrited all day by a pack of naughty children. Just tell me what you're doing with this 'ere bottle, and then be off with you.'

Matilda once more approached her lips to the trumpet, but this time she took care not to shout.

'We thought you would like some whisky, so we brought it as a present.'

'Who told you I liked whisky?' said the old man, and his eyes gleamed fiercely under his shaggy eyebrows.

'Nobody told us.'

'I'll learn you whether I like whisky or not,' said the old man, getting up with the bottle in his hand. 'I'm a going to learn you a lesson you'll never forget. You brought me whisky to drink, did you?'

'Yes,' faltered Matilda, wishing most fervently that she had done nothing of the kind.

'Very well,' said the old man; 'you see this here open winder looking onto my garden?'

The children looked at it and at him in silence.

'You can go back to them as sent you,' said the old man angrily, 'and tell 'em as Joshua Grute has been a teetotaller for nine-and-forty year, and that he ain't going to be tempted into bad ways at his time of life,' and he raised his arm, struck an attitude of noble indignation, and flung the bottle violently out of the window.

There was a crash and a scream.

The old man seemed to crumple up suddenly, and collapsed into a little heap in his chair. He still held his trumpet to his ear.

'What are you doing, Joshua, a-throwing things at me like that?' cried a shrill voice.

'I – I – didn't know you was there, Joanna,' said the old man quite meekly.

'Don't tell *me* as you didn't know I was digging in the pertater bed,' cried the voice, 'when you hit the very spade I'm digging with, and splashed me all over with liquor and broken glass. Why, you might have killed me. Just you wait half a moment and I'll let you know what I think of you.'

'Run, Caroline, run; she's coming!' said Matilda, in an agony; and she seized the basket, and fled after her sister, both of them being so frightened that they never stopped till they found themselves at the other end of the village.

'Oh dear, oh dear. How very unpleasant it was. I wish we'd asked Aunt Emily to come with us,' said Caroline. 'She *said* it required tact and experience to visit the poor.'

'Nothing of the kind,' said obstinate Matilda. 'You are always ready to give in directly. How could we possibly tell that horrid old man was a teetotaller? I shall try again somewhere else.'

'Don't let it be another old man,' entreated Caroline.

'It's very unlikely that there is an old man in every cottage,' said Matilda. 'But this time, Caroline, I shall remember that appearances are deceitful, and I shall *not* choose a pretty cottage. I went in there simply because it was so tidy, and I fancy tidy people are generally cross. Nanny is tidy. We will choose the poorest looking cottage we can see this time.'

There was a small wretched cottage at the end of the street, standing some way back from the road. The gate of the garden was off its hinges, the path was covered with weeds, and a broken window-pane was stuffed with rags.

'They must be *very* poor,' said Matilda. 'I will give them my packet of tea.'

'Where *did* you get that?' said Caroline, looking admiringly at the neat newspaper parcel she produced.

'I emptied the tea caddy into the *Evening Standard*,' said Matilda with pride.

This time a quavering voice cried 'Come in!' when they knocked, and they found an old woman sitting in a patchwork elbow chair by a rickety table.

There was no fire in this grate, and the room looked as though it had not been cleaned for days. The old woman matched the room, and the atmosphere was unpleasantly close and stuffy.

'Come in, deary,' said the old woman.

Matilda was determined not to be mistaken again for a little girl trying to sell something, so she began at once:

'We come from Finch Hall, and we've brought you some nice tea as a present.'

'I don't never touch tea, deary,' said the old woman. 'The doctor says it would kill me. If it was a drop of brandy now . . .'

'Oh dear me, how very unfortunate!' said Caroline.

'We had a bottle of whisky just now,' said Matilda, 'but Joshua Grute threw it out of the window.'

'Just like him,' said the old woman. 'Couldn't you get a drop more, deary?'

Somehow Matilda liked this old woman even less than cross old Joshua Grute. She had a most unpleasant leer when she smiled.

'I dare say I *could* tomorrow,' said Matilda doubtfully. 'There is plenty in the cellar, and I'm sure Papa wouldn't grudge it if you're too poor to buy it for yourself.'

'I haven't a penny in the world, lovey,' said the old woman. 'And I haven't had a drop of spirit in this house for months. It's the only thing that does my complaint good, too. The doctor says I ought to live on it. But I can't stir from this chair to get it for myself.'

'I'll bring you some tomorrow,' said Matilda.

'There's a little love!' said the old woman. 'Don't say a word to nobody, but just bring it along under your pinny. Martha Otton's my name. What else have you got in your basket, deary?'

She was just beginning to fumble in the basket, which Caroline was resting on the table, when the door-latch was lifted and a brisk little girl of about fifteen came in.

'Mother's sent me to tidy you up, Granny.'

'Go away, Bella,' said Martha Otton; 'I've got visitors.'

'Well, I wouldn't let visitors in to see the place in such a state. I'm ashamed of you, Granny, that I am. You've been drinking again,' said Bella.

She looked round the room with her sharp little eyes, and pounced on a black bottle in the corner. 'You've been out to the public-house and got more spirits, after promising mother you wouldn't.'

'Why, she said she hadn't had any in the house for months!' cried Caroline.

'Don't you believe her, Miss.'

'But if it's the only thing that does her good,' said Matilda doubtfully, 'you oughtn't to grudge it to her. And I told her I would ask Papa to send her a bottle of whisky tomorrow.'

'Send Granny whisky!' cried Bella, in a voice of horror, 'when me and mother is doing all we know to keep her from taking a drop too much every day of her life. You surely wouldn't never play us such a trick as that. Why, she's had more than's good for her now.'

'Don't say nothing to nobody, deary,' said the old woman, and she fell asleep in her chair with a foolish smile on her face.

'I won't ask you to sit down,' said Bella, 'for I've got to clean the place up, and wash and dress Granny.'

Matilda and Caroline felt that they could not ignore this very broad hint, so they picked up their basket and bade Bella good afternoon in rather sheepish tones.

'I don't think this is a very nice village, so far,' said Caroline in trembling tones as they walked away.

'Nonsense, leave it to me,' said Matilda, who never acknowledged herself in the wrong if she could possibly help it. 'Of course, if we had known that Martha Otton was inclined to be tipsy we would have avoided her.'

'And if we had known Joshua Grute was a teetotaller we should have avoided *him*,' said poor Caroline, rather puzzled. 'I do hope we shall be luckier next time, Matilda.'

They now paused before a very small cottage indeed, semi-detached, with a fly-blown card in the window on which was inscribed 'Miss Rowe, dressmaker'.

'This looks very respectable,' said Matilda encouragingly.

Here there was a knocker and a bell, and after a very long delay the door was opened by a tall, elderly lady with ringlets on each side of her face, and a large cameo brooch fastening a lace collar on her black silk dress.

Matilda was holding out a small packet of lump sugar (which she had removed from the breakfast table that morning) all ready for her acceptance but she felt it to be an inappropriate offering for this dignified personage, and stood abashed by the side of Caroline, who clutched her covered basket and remained as speechless as her sister.

'We don't want anything today, thank you,' said Miss Rowe, in majestic tones which matched her appearance, and she shut the door in their faces.

'Another failure,' said Caroline dismally.

'Not at all,' said Matilda bravely. 'The loss is hers. I *meant*, when I saw what a very superior person she was, to give her the little Dresden statuette off the drawing-room mantelpiece.'

'Did Papa say you might have that?' said Caroline, astonished.

'He said he wished there were not so many ornaments, only the other day, when he couldn't find room to put down a cup of tea,' said Matilda, 'so I cleared away one or two simply to please him.'

'The basket is still heavy,' said Caroline.

'Those are Cissie's and William's and Emily's playthings,' said Matilda. 'Mamma said they were growing too old for toys, so I went quietly to the nursery cupboard and took them away. Let us go into *this* house, Caroline. There is a child looking out of the window.'

Caroline assented joyfully, and this time it really seemed as though they had made no mistake, for a grinning urchin of eight opened the door, and five little boys and girls crowded eagerly around. As they were all very small, Matilda and Caroline felt as superior and grown-up as possible, and sat down in two kitchen chairs, with the basket between them.

'What is your name, dear?' said Matilda condescendingly to the biggest child.

'Polly,' said the biggest child.

'And what is your mother's name?'

'Mizzis Tompkins.'

'Would you like some toys, Polly?' said Matilda.

'Yes'm,' said Polly.

Matilda then generously distributed her brother and sisters' toys among the little Tompkinses, and Clumsy Caroline was so pleased with their delight that she could not help turning the basket upside down to see if any more surprises would drop out for them. The only things left were the Dresden china ornaments from the drawing-room mantelpiece, and they fell on the tiles and were broken to pieces.

Matilda was annoyed for a moment, but she quickly forgot her vexation in the pleasure of feeding the little Tompkinses with lumps of sugar.

'Please, miss, ain't you got nothing for Billy?' said Polly.

'You've *each* got something; don't be greedy, Polly,' said Matilda, with dignity.

'Billy's upstairs – he's ill in bed,' said Polly. 'That's why we wasn't let to go to school. He's got the measles.'

'Oh, Matilda, what *will* Mamma say?' said Caroline, for she remembered that when measles broke out at the Academy for Young Gentlemen the boys had not been allowed to go near the school for weeks.

'It isn't as if we'd *seen* Billy,' said Matilda, feeling a little uncomfortable. 'However, perhaps we'd better not stop any longer.'

She hurried Caroline away as quickly as possible, and the children were too much engrossed with their new playthings even to say goodbye.

'Where are we going now, Matilda?' said Caroline, who was growing tired.

Matilda was just going to say 'Home,' when she caught sight of two tramps moving slowly towards them.

'Oh, Caroline, here are *really* poor people,' she said. 'What a pity we've given everything away.'

'They don't look very *nice* tramps,' said Caroline doubtfully.

'How can they look nice in such dirty old rags?' said Matilda. 'I tell you what, Caroline: we will take them home with us and offer them a really good tea, and get Golightly to give them some of Papa's old clothes.'

Caroline was delighted with the idea, and Matilda walked boldly up to the tramps.

'Might I offer you a little refreshment?' she said kindly. 'You look tired and thirsty.'

The tramps looked first at Matilda and then at each other; then the big tramp winked at the little tramp, which offended Matilda, but she supposed he knew no better.

'I'll take a pint of four 'arf, miss,' he said in a husky tone, and wiped his mouth with the back of his hand.

'I don't know if we *have* any four 'arf,' said Matilda, 'but I dare say the cook would be able to make it for you, if you would like to come home and have tea with my sister and me. We live in that big house over there. And if you would *care* to accept a few clothes,' she said as delicately as she could, 'we should be pleased to give you some.'

The tramps looked at each other again.

'Thank you, miss,' said the husky tramp; 'but what would yer par and mar say, I wonder?'

'They are out driving, as it happens,' said Matilda, 'so they won't say anything; and if – if you don't like meeting the servants, who *are* a little stuck up,' she added considerately, 'we could take you in through the drawing-room window, and bring you whatever you like without your seeing anybody at all.'

'Could you, now?' said the husky tramp. 'Me and my mate is very much obliged to you, ain't we, Bill?'

The mate said nothing, but he put the black pipe he had been smoking into his pocket, and buttoned his ragged jacket across his chest.

'Follow me,' said Matilda, in a flutter of importance; 'I will take you a short cut through the park.'

Enchanted with her charitable intentions, she started off at such a pace that the tramps had some ado to keep up with her, and they all presently arrived, quite unperceived, in the shrubbery.

Here Matilda requested her guests to remain hidden among the bushes until she had reconnoitred. Finding no one about, she returned to their hiding place, and brought them triumphantly into the drawing-room through the open window.

'While you are resting,' she said, 'I will go and get you a tray of refreshments with my own hands, and my sister will go to my father's dressing-room and bring you down some boots and some nice new clothes, which I am sure you need very badly. We won't be long.'

'Take your time, miss,' said the husky tramp; 'we kin wait.'

Matilda nodded to them both graciously, and hurried away with Caroline, who was quite as much excited and pleased as she was herself.

She went to the still-room to find Margery, and begged her for a tray of cakes and a jug of milk for some visitors who had just arrived.

'Visitors! What visitors? Your Papa and Mamma haven't come in yet,' said Margery.

'These are – acquaintances of my own,' said Matilda; 'two poor tramps, to whom I have offered refreshment.'

'Where are they?' said Margery.

'In the drawing-room.'

'Tramps in the drawing-room!' screamed Margery. 'We shall all be murdered in our beds this night. Golightly, Golightly! Help!'

Her cries brought the other servants to the still-room, and, in spite of Matilda's indignant protests, Golightly caught up the poker, and the butler and footmen followed him upstairs and into the drawing-room.

There was not a tramp to be seen.

'You have frightened them away,' sobbed Matilda.

'Where's my silver table? As I thought, cleared of every single thing, gold snuff-boxes and all,' said the butler, wringing his hands.

'The turquoise writing-set is gone,' said the first footman.

'The candlesticks off the desk have disappeared,' cried the second footman.

Matilda, thunderstruck, stood in the middle of the room and wept.

'There's the front door bell. The master and missis is home,' said Golightly, and hurried away.

Mr Chubb, on hearing the news, immediately despatched the servants to ring the alarm bell and give chase to the thieves, while Aunt Emily sat on the sofa and bewailed the loss of her gold thimble, which had gone with the rest.

Mrs Chubb sent Margery to make sure that the twins had not been kidnapped again.

'Perhaps, Matilda, you will now be good enough to explain your conduct,' said her father.

Matilda was just about to begin when Caroline, who had heard none of the commotion, tripped joyfully into the room with her arms full of Mr Chubb's clothes, which she had collected from his wardrobe, and now threw down triumphantly on the floor at his feet.

'Have you taken leave of your senses, Caroline?' cried Mr Chubb, recognising his best evening suit, varnished shoes, and new silk socks.

'They were for the tramps, Papa,' sobbed Matilda. 'You told us we must not be selfish in our good fortune.'

'Did I tell Caroline to give away *my* things?' said Mr Chubb.

'It was my fault, not Caroline's,' said Matilda, weeping still more bitterly, and she recounted the whole of her foolish behaviour to her pained and astonished parents.

One result of her narrative was that she and Caroline were kept in strict quarantine for a fortnight, in case they should have caught the measles, which, however, fortunately proved not to be the case; and another was that Matilda's pocket money was confiscated for three months in order to replace the toys which she had arbitrarily taken from her brother and sisters' toy cupboard, and thus she learnt that there was small merit in being generous at other people's expense.

Another result was that Mr Chubb had to complain no more of the superabundance of ornaments in the drawing-room, for the gold and silver articles stolen by the tramps were not recovered, and the tramps themselves were never heard of again.

7

AT THE FLOWER SHOW

Mrs Chubb had often observed that Clumsy Caroline, Selfish
Cissie, and Greedy George received less notice from strangers
than their brothers and sisters, and as she was very tender-hearted,
she desired to make them amends, so she proposed that these
three should be chosen to accompany their parents and aunt to
the Flower Show at Burridge; and Mr Chubb agreed on condition
that Miss Jenkins should come with them.

Caroline, Cissie, and George were delighted to hear of their
good fortune, and were all ready, dressed in their best, waiting
to enter the wagonette with Miss Jenkins at the appointed hour.

'On our way to the show you had better call at the rectory, my love,' said Mr Chubb to his wife. 'It is quite a week since the Woolaways called upon us last.'

'But Mrs Woolaway will be at the Flower Show,' objected Mrs Chubb.

'That is the reason I suggest you should take this opportunity of calling, Maria,' said Mr Chubb. 'You know it fatigues you to get in and out of the carriage, and at the same time I do not like you to neglect our neighbours. In this manner you will be able to show civility to Mrs Woolaway without any fatigue at all either to yourself or to her. That is my plan.'

Unfortunately for Mr Chubb's plan, Mrs Woolaway had that morning sprained her ankle, and thus was unable to go to the Flower Show; so when the Chubb footman inquired of the Woolaway parlour-maid whether her mistress was at home, the answer was in the affirmative.

'Now we shall be late for the opening, and as the Duchess of Pontypool was to open the show, I particularly wanted to see it,' said poor Mrs Chubb.

'You need not stay long,' said Mr Chubb, disconcerted. 'Take one of the children in with you; they can get in and out of the carriage more quickly than Emily or myself.'

As though to illustrate his words, no sooner had the footman opened the door of the wagonette than Clumsy Caroline missed her footing, and taking only one step to the ground, rolled under the carriage, from whence the servant extricated her with some difficulty.

Poor Mrs Chubb, who followed, dusted her daughter as well as she could with her pocket-handkerchief, the footman bent her hat into shape, and they hastened into the rectory, and were announced by the giggling parlourmaid, who had witnessed Caroline's sudden descent from the carriage.

Mrs Woolaway was spread carefully out upon the sofa, covered with a shawl, and she begged Mrs Chubb to excuse her for being unable to move.

'I am afraid you will have a very hot drive into Burridge,' she said, 'and you look tired already, dear Mrs Chubb. Do allow me to order you a cup of tea.'

Mrs Chubb protested that she had only just had luncheon, and that she did not want any tea; but as Mrs Woolaway persisted, she gave way, and the bell was rung.

'I am very sorry you cannot come to the Flower Show,' she said politely.

'So am I,' said Mrs Woolaway. 'I hear your fruit is quite wonderful; the peaches the biggest that ever were seen. I hope you will get a prize.'

'I hope we may,' said Mrs Chubb; 'but to tell you the truth, I have not even seen the peaches. Jones the gardener keeps all the houses locked up, and he is such a disagreeable man I am afraid to go near him. I hope *you* will get a prize for your beautiful roses.'

'I hope we may,' said Mrs Woolaway.

'What very fine china you have!' said Mrs Chubb, looking round the room in search of something pleasant to say.

'I am sure you are very kind; we have nothing so good as our tea-set,' said Mrs Woolaway, beaming. 'Here it is, and I hope you will admire *that*, for the cups are Sèvres.'

'It is very fine indeed,' said Mrs Chubb; 'almost too good to use.'

'Oh, but we take *such* care of it,' said Mrs Woolaway, and she poured some tea out for her visitor from a most delicate china teapot.

Caroline, who was a very willing child, sprang from her chair and started forward to take the cup from her hostess and hand it to her mamma; but alas! scarcely had she touched it when she caught her foot in the fringe of the Kidderminster carpet. Vainly endeavouring to save herself from falling, she clutched at the light tea-table, and upset it so heavily that the china tea-service was scattered in every direction; the bread and butter lay face downwards on the mat, the tea streamed over Caroline's new frock, and Mrs Woolaway, forgetting all about her sprained ankle, ran hither and thither distractedly, picking up stray pieces of cups and saucers and trying to fit them together; while Mrs Chubb, bursting into tears, asked herself repeatedly why Caroline had ever been born.

'It doesn't matter in the *least*,' said Mrs Woolaway, in a high and unnaturally cheerful key, recovering her presence of mind. 'After all, it is only four cups and saucers, and I have a dozen – and the teapot was of a different pattern. I am only concerned that you should have to wait while they bring some fresh tea.'

'Not another moment will I keep Caroline here,' said Mrs Chubb, rising in great agitation. 'My only object now is to get her safely out of the house before she can do any further mischief,' and in spite of Mrs Woolaway's kind protestations, she led Caroline firmly from the room and back to the wagonette, where she explained to Mr Chubb what had happened.

'If you will allow me,' said Miss Jenkins, 'I will conduct Caroline home on foot immediately. It is clearly impossible that she can go to the Flower Show in her present condition.'

'It seems very hard, Miss Jenkins, that you should lose your outing because Caroline has been careless.'

But Miss Jenkins assured her employer so warmly that she preferred walking to driving, that Mr Chubb consented to let her take Caroline home.

'And kindly send her to bed the instant you arrive. Such clumsiness cannot pass unpunished,' said Caroline's father, disregarding his daughter's noisy sobs.

'Oh, Papa, Papa, Mrs Woolaway says our peaches are sure to get a prize. I want to see them. Surely you can't have the heart to send me to bed.'

'If you will excuse me, I had far rather give her a lesson to learn; she knows next to nothing, and is only too fond of her bed,' said Miss Jenkins; and poor Caroline was marched away in disgrace.

'Do not be distressed, Maria,' said Mr Chubb. 'We are fortunately now in a position to repair the disaster which has arisen through our child's carelessness. As soon as we get home I will send Mrs Woolaway one of the best Dresden tea-sets from the china closet.'

'I am very glad you will do that, Thomas,' said Mrs Chubb, 'but I cannot help feeling all in a tremble. It seems so odd that I cannot even pay a simple call without some accident or another.'

While Mr Chubb and Aunt Emily devoted themselves to cheering Mrs Chubb, Greedy George and Selfish Cissie conversed with one another apart in the corner of the wagonette.

'I can't help feeling sorry for Caroline. After all, it was an accident,' said George, who, in spite of his greediness, was a kind-hearted boy.

'It serves her right,' said Cissie. 'She is *always* having accidents;

and besides, George, I'm rather glad this has happened, for now we shall be able to enjoy ourselves, which would have been quite impossible with Miss Jenkins saying "Don't do that, dear," every moment.'

'I don't believe there's much fun at a flower show after all,' said George, 'if it's only walking about and looking at a lot of silly flowers.

'Oh dear me, you can do far nicer things than that,' said Cissie. 'There are Aunt Sallies, and coconut shies, and merry-go-rounds. Molly's new young man is a soldier in the band and he told her all about it; and Molly and Golightly and Margery are all coming together in the evening.'

'I've spent my last week's pocket-money on toffee,' said George gloomily. 'I shan't be able to ride the merry-go-round horses, or shy at the coconuts, or anything. Can you lend me something, Cissie?'

'You know I make it a rule never to lend anything,' said Selfish Cissie, tossing her pigtail. 'But I tell you what I *will* do for you, George. I am very fond of coconuts, and I have brought my satchel to carry away any I may happen to win.'

'*You* win!' said George derisively. 'Why, you can't even throw and you couldn't hit a haystack.'

'I never said I was a good shot,' said Cissie, with her nose in the air. 'Ladies have no *need* to throw – especially when they have money.' She drew out her purse with great dignity. 'I will pay for you to have six shots, George; they are three a penny; and if you win any coconuts of course they must belong to *me*.'

'You mean cat!' said George, disgusted.

Cissie put her purse away.

'Very well, I can easily get somebody else to do it.'

'No, no, I'll do it,' grumbled George, who reflected that the sport of throwing would be better than nothing.

'I suppose you'll let me have a bit. You can't eat a whole coconut,' he said sulkily.

'*I* am not greedy,' said Cissie pointedly.

For some time they did not speak to each other again. But when the wagonette drew up before the field in which the Flower Show was being held, and the children saw the palisade decorated with flags, the crowd passing in through the barriers, and the large tents dotted about on the grass, and heard the band playing above all the noise of talking and laughter and shouting, they forgot their squabble and became excited.

'Keep together, children, and follow me,' said Mr Chubb fussily, 'or you will be lost in the crowd.'

'I had no idea there would be so many people,' said Mrs Chubb, clinging to her husband's arm.

'It is only just about the entrance, my love,' said Mr Chubb soothingly. 'We will go straight to the tents to look at Jones's exhibits. I hope we have won a prize or two, after all the money the gardens cost.'

'It is to be hoped you have, Thomas,' said Aunt Emily, who was growing rather cross with the heat, 'since Jones has made this show the excuse for sending next to no fruit into the house.'

'It is more important that our fruit should take a good place in the exhibition than that we should eat it, Emily,' said Mr Chubb reprovingly.

'There are the Aunt Sallies, George,' whispered Cissie. 'Let us slip away as soon as we can. I have my little satchel all ready, and twopence in my hand.'

At this moment the Duke and Duchess of Pontypool, escorted by the Mayor and Corporation, appeared on the scene; and Mr and Mrs Chubb and Aunt Emily all hastened forward to see and be seen. Cissie and George were therefore able to slip away quite easily towards the amusement booths.

Here Cissie produced her two pennies, and George had six shies; but alas! he did not succeed in hitting a single thing.

'Let me try once more,' he said in crestfallen tones.

'Certainly not,' said Cissie angrily. 'I've wasted twopence already.'

Poor George vainly turned his pockets inside out, hoping to find a forgotten halfpenny, and he was just moving away from the booth with a sigh when Admiral Plumpton suddenly clapped him on the shoulder and cried in a hearty tone:

'The little fisherman, hey? I saw you arrive with your father. Let's see what you can do! Have a shilling's worth, hey?'

George assented with delight, and shied with all his might, and such was the effect of the Admiral's encouragement that presently half a dozen coconuts fell to his share.

'We don't want 'em, hey?' said the Admiral, prepared to hand them back to the expectant attendant.

'Oh, if you please!' shrieked Cissie, and she started forward with her little satchel, 'I brought this on purpose for them.'

'Bless me,' said the Admiral, 'is this your sister? Well, well; get in as many as you can, and put back the rest. And now I'll give you a turn on the merry-go-round.'

Cissie got three coconuts into her bag, and George took one under his arm; and they then climbed on to the wooden horses and had ride after ride, until the Admiral's wife came and took him away.

'What shall we do now?' said George.

'Come and look at the peaches Caroline talked about,' said Cissie.

'What's the good of looking at them when we shan't be allowed to taste them?' said George.

'Perhaps we *shall* be allowed,' said Cissie, who thought it very unlikely, but reflected that the hope would draw George back towards the fashionable end of the show, where, being very vain, she was now anxious to exhibit her new frock.

They entered one of the largest tents.

'It's like an oven,' said George, disgusted. 'Let's stay outside.'

'No, no; look at the fruit,' said Cissie, and she pointed at a dish of nectarines on a table next the entrance, with a large card leaning against it, inscribed 'Third Prize'.

'Just think what the first prize must be,' said George. 'Come on in at once,' and he made haste to follow Cissie.

Dish after dish of exquisite fruit met his hungry eyes; and as though to make them yet more irresistible, large slices had been cut from the melons, to show the fresh, rose-coloured flesh of the interior.

'How dull it makes those old coconuts seem,' grumbled ungrateful Cissie, 'and they're frightfully heavy to carry too!'

'I'm so hot and thirsty,' sighed George.

At this moment a bell rang outside, and everybody began to crowd towards the entrance of the tent.

'What's going to happen?' said a young lady behind George.

'The Duke of Pontypool is going to make a speech. Come along, my dear,' said her mother.

'Come along, George,' echoed Cissie.

'*I* don't want to hear speeches,' said George. 'Look here, Cissie. What a shame! Why, it's *our* peaches and nectarines and melons that have the first prizes. "Exhibited by Mr Jones, head gardener at Finch Hall." I do call this beastly cheek. Old Jones getting first prizes, and us locked out of our own greenhouses, and not allowed to touch anything but the scrubbiest little ones he can find. I have a very good mind to eat one. It can't be stealing, as it's our own.'

'There is a policeman at the entrance. Suppose he saw you. *He'd* think you were stealing,' said Cissie doubtfully.

'He can't see us here,' said George, for they were now alone at the extreme end of the tent, and there was a high bank of palms and ferns running down the centre, which concealed the entrance from their view.

'I tell you what I'll do,' said George. 'There are seven peaches on this dish. I'll take a bite off the top one, and you shall take another, and then we'll put it back with the bites underneath.'

'Nonsense!' said Cissie. 'A nice mess the juice will make of our clothes and the dish too. A much better plan would be to get rid of the stupid coconuts in my bag and fill it up with peaches. As you say, they really *belong* to us. And if I take one very carefully off each dish, no one will be any the wiser.'

George approved of this plan so much that he willingly hid the three coconuts among the pots in the fern bank, while Cissie, who was very neat-fingered, extracted seven peaches, and re-arranged the dishes so skilfully that no one would have perceived they had been touched.

'Let's go off somewhere and eat them at once,' said Greedy George.

'We can't eat them till we get home,' said Cissie.

'But I'm so thirsty,' urged George.

'You are a very greedy boy,' said Cissie, and she walked out of the tent with her bag in her hand and her little nose in the air, past the unsuspecting policeman, supposing George would follow her.

But George could not tear himself away from the fruit. He looked and longed. At last the temptation became so strong that he lifted a slice of his father's largest melon, and tasted it with the tip of his tongue. It refreshed him so much that he took a bite, and when he replaced it on the dish the bite seemed so conspicuous that he thought he might as well finish the slice and be done with it. So he finished it. Then he reflected that the passers-by could see the inside of the melons better without the cut slices in the way, so he finished them all, and hid the rinds among the fern. By this time he was tired of melon, and growing bolder with success, determined to slip one peach from a dish, as Cissie had done, and eat it. Being so very greedy, he naturally chose the biggest and ripest he could see, and having peeled off the red velvet skin of the sunny side, he applied it to his mouth.

He liked the peach so much better than the melon, and it was so deliciously sweet, that he took another, and after that another, till the top dish was empty; and he thought he had better slip it underneath one of the full ones, rather than attempt to fill it by robbing the other dishes.

As he was endeavouring to do so, however, there was a tremendous outburst of clapping and cheering outside, and George was so startled that he upset the dish he was lifting, and the peaches rolled off it across the table and onto the grass beneath. George stooped to pick them up, and as he got up, very red and frightened, with a peach in each hand, he came face to face with the policeman.

'Now, young gentleman, I've caught you!' said the policeman. 'No use for you to go denying of it. You've got your mouth full of peach at this very moment.'

'They're my father's peaches,' said George in great terror.

'Ah, indeed!' said the policeman. 'We'll come before the Mayor this very minute, and hear what he has to say about that.'

Opposite the entrance of the tent from which the policeman now emerged, holding George by the collar, was a small platform. On the platform was the Duke making a speech, and the Duchess waiting till he had done, to distribute the prizes. Consequently poor George found himself the centre of observation, and a sorry object he looked, crimson with shame and fright, with juice running down his clean collar and blue necktie, and a peach-stone bulging out his right cheek, while he still clutched a peach in either hand and held his coconut under his arm. The Duke paused in his speech, there was first a dead silence, and then a roar of laughter.

The only people who did not laugh were poor Mr and Mrs

Chubb, who were horrified at the spectacle presented by their son; and Selfish Cissie, who crept close to Aunt Emily in a great fright lest she too should be discovered, though she knew that George would not tell of her if he could help it.

'What's this, what's this?' cried the Mayor, bustling up. 'Has this bad little boy been stealing the peaches?'

'They're our own peaches,' sobbed George. 'Go and look if you don't believe me. Every one of them came from Finch Hall. I wouldn't have touched them else. I'm not a thief. I only wanted to taste them because the gardener kept them locked up.'

Here he suddenly turned purple in the face, and began to choke and splutter violently.

'He's swallowed the stone!' screamed his mother.

A great confusion now ensued. George was held upside down by the Mayor and the policeman, and thumped and shaken and punched in turn. At last, to everyone's relief, the stone dropped out of his mouth, and he was then reversed, and handed over to Mrs Chubb, weeping bitterly; while Mr Chubb explained matters to the Mayor, withdrew all claims to the prizes he had won, and promised to give his son a sound thrashing before he was a day older.

After this painful episode, of course it was quite impossible for any of the family to enjoy the Flower Show, and on the first opportunity they all made their way out of the enclosure, found the wagonette, and drove home again as fast as they could, George frightened and sulky, Mr Chubb silent and angry, Aunt Emily stating over and over again that she knew it from the first, and Mrs Chubb in tears. Cissie sat alone in her corner, clutching her bag in a fright, and expecting every moment that somebody would ask her what it contained. But nobody did, and as soon as they reached the hall, she flew up to the nursery and hid the peaches in her doll's cradle, resolving to eat them as soon as she found a chance.

Meantime Mr Chubb gave George a sound whipping and sent him to his room, where Charles and William presently came to condole with him. But their condolences turned to disgust when he related his story.

'If you'd taken them *here*, I should have thought nothing of it in comparison, but to go disgracing yourself in public!' said Charles. 'I would thrash you myself, George, if father hadn't.'

'You wouldn't if you knew how ill I felt,' sobbed George.

'Did you tell father about Cissie?'

'Of course not, and luckily he didn't ask a single question.'

'How many peaches did you eat?'

'Seven or eight,' groaned George, 'and I forget how many slices of melon. I never wish to see a peach again as long as I live.'

'And how many had Cissie in the bag?'

'I didn't count. Oh, oh, oh!' sobbed George.

'And she never said a word, and let *you* get all the blame?' said Charles.

'It was my idea,' said George. 'She only helped, and she didn't eat any. They *were* our own peaches; the Mayor said if they hadn't been he'd have had to send me to prison. Oh dear, oh dear.'

'A nice disgrace that would have been for us all,' said Charles. 'Well, you won't be so greedy in future, George. I'll send Nanny to you, as you seem to be rather bad. Come on, William.' and they left George to his repentance and the tender offices of Nanny, who presently came and administered to him a large dose of the nastiest medicine he had ever tasted.

Charles and William took the opportunity of Nanny's absence to go to the nursery, where they found Dorothea reading and sharp little Emily playing marbles with Caroline.

'Where's Cissie?' said Charles.

'She's gone to change her best frock,' said Emily.

'Has she been here?'

'Only for a moment. She went to her toy cupboard and put away her satchel, and played with her doll's cradle for a minute or two,' said Emily.

Charles immediately went to the toy cupboard, and there found the empty satchel hanging on a peg, while William turned the doll's cradle upside down.

Out rolled seven magnificent peaches.

'Now I'll tell you what we'll do. We won't tell tales,' said Charles, 'but we'll pay Miss Cissie out for leaving poor George to suffer all by himself, when she was just as bad as he was.'

So they ate all the peaches, and when they had finished Charles made a neat parcel of the seven stones, and wrote outside, 'A present for a mean little pig'.

This he put carefully away in the doll's cradle, and forbidding his brother and sisters ever to mention the subject to Cissie, he went downstairs and told George what he had done.

Cissie no doubt discovered the trick that had been played upon her, for she appeared at tea with red eyes; but as she could not complain to anyone without disclosing her own misdoings, she was obliged to put up with her punishment in silence; and she incurred a further penalty for her misdeeds in the course of the evening, for Nanny observed her throwing a parcel into the nursery grate, and discovering seven stones inside it, made up her mind that Cissie had eaten seven peaches; and as nothing would induce her to believe Cissie's protestations to the contrary, she gave her then and there a large dose of the same medicine that she had already administered to George.

8

THE DRIVE TO THE
CASTLE

Early one morning a special messenger arrived at Finch Hall with
a note from the Duchess.

The contents were as follows:

DEAR MRS CHUBB, It would give us much pleasure if you and
Mr Chubb and Miss Finch would come over today. General
Benjamin Finch is coming to luncheon at one; the half-brother,
as no doubt you know, of your late cousin, Mr Joseph Finch. He

has expressed a desire to meet you. Pray bring dear little William with you, and, in case he should be dull by himself, let him invite one of his sisters to accompany him.

Yours sincerely,

SOPHIA PONTYPOOL

The Duchess liked the latest fashion in notepaper, so she wrote on a single sheet of vellum-like substance nearly a foot square, and filled it with her enormous handwriting; but though her writing was large it was not distinct, and though she underlined the word *today* four times, both Mr and Mrs Chubb and Aunt Emily (who read the invitation joyfully over and over again) always read *to stay* instead of *today*.

'Well, this *is* kind,' said Mr Chubb.

'I had no idea Cousin Joseph *had* a half-brother,' said Aunt Emily.

'The lawyer told me that he had quarrelled with him in early youth and forbidden anyone to mention his name, so I said nothing about him,' said Mr Chubb.

'It must have been in Benjamin's early youth,' said Aunt Emily.

'I said so,' said Mr Chubb crossly.

'But I fear we are keeping the poor man out of his lawful inheritance,' said Mrs Chubb.

'Nonsense, Maria! How can that be when Cousin Joseph made all his money in potted lobsters?' argued Mr Chubb. 'However, if he is badly off, he has only to say so, and my purse will be at his service.'

Mrs Chubb could not help admiring her husband, and shed tears of thankfulness as she clearly perceived that the sudden acquisition of riches had not in the least impaired his native generosity.

'In going to stay at such a *very* large house, my love,' said Mr Chubb, 'it will be necessary to take a few retainers.'

'What can you mean, Thomas?' said Mrs Chubb, astonished.

'I mean, Maria, that we must not go to the castle unattended,' said Mr Chubb firmly. 'It is due to our position, as well as to the Duke and Duchess, that we should arrive with a proper suite. I propose that Margery should accompany us to wait upon you and Emily, and Molly as maid to whichever of our daughters we decide to take with us. Golightly will valet me, and Mr Higginbotham must attend us to look after William and keep an eye on Golightly, who, as you know, is not entirely to be trusted, though it would break the faithful fellow's heart were we to leave him behind. Miss Jenkins besides must certainly come, for she has plenty of common sense, and will make sure that William plays no monkey tricks upon poor Mr Higginbotham.'

'You know best, Thomas,' said his wife; 'but will not the Duke and Duchess be surprised to see ten people arrive instead of five?'

'No, my love,' said her husband. 'They do not trouble themselves about such details.'

'All I can say is that I think it very absurd,' said Aunt Emily; 'and you need not take Margery on my account, for I have always waited on myself, and always shall.'

'Emily,' said Mr Chubb mildly, 'I am acquainted with the interiors of grand establishments, and you are not. I have been twice over Windsor Castle; besides which, Mrs Woolaway informs me that when the Duchess of Pontypool pays a visit she takes with her a maid, a secretary, a companion, a hospital nurse, a footman, four little dogs, and a canary bird. Why then should she suppose five retainers too many for our five selves?'

'But if everyone is coming with us, Thomas, who is to look after the children who remain at home?' objected Mrs Chubb.

'Nanny is quite equal to looking after everything and everybody, my love,' said Mr Chubb decidedly. 'Now let us have no more discussion. We have little time to lose. We must break the news of our immediate departure to the household and order our best clothes to be packed at once.'

'How long shall we stay, Thomas?'

'Well, the Duchess very kindly leaves that an open question,' said Mr Chubb, after carefully re-reading the invitation from beginning to end. 'I should say not more than a week at the outside; possibly ten days if we are enjoying ourselves very much or if they seem at all reluctant to let us go.'

'It will be impossible for me to stay more than six days, Thomas, for I have only six evening-dresses, and I could not wear the same gown twice,' said Aunt Emily firmly. 'Even *that* includes a tea-gown much the worse for wear, and my best velvet dress, which still smells very strongly of sherry.'

'Don't be ridiculous, Emily. What can it matter to the Duke and Duchess what you wear. They will probably not notice your dress at all,' said Mr Chubb severely.

'I do not care a fig for the Duke and Duchess. Of course they won't care what I wear, what does it matter to them?' said Aunt Emily scornfully. 'I am only thinking of what the servants would say.'

'You will not hear what their servants say, Emily.'

'But I shall know they are saying it, all the same,' said Aunt Emily triumphantly.

As Mr Chubb was well aware Aunt Emily would always have the last word, he said no more, but hurried away to order the wagonette for themselves and the brake for the servants and luggage.

All was now bustle and confusion. Wilful William was told of his good luck, and immediately chose sharp little Emily to accompany him; Mr Higginbotham got out his Gladstone bag and filled it with necessaries to the very brim, and Miss Jenkins slipped a few lesson-books and a small pair of globes into her trunk, resolved that she would lose no opportunity of improving Emily's mind during the visit.

Since inheriting her fortune, Mrs Chubb had given *carte blanche* to an artistic firm of children's outfitters to send fancy clothes suited to the various ages and sizes of her offspring, and consequently the variety of her children's costumes was amazing. On this occasion Emily was dressed in the latest Dutch fashion, while William wore a green suit like an early English woodman. He objected less than usual to being dressed up, however, because the suit included a nice little horn to be slung over the shoulder and a toy hunting knife in the belt.

'If we *should* meet any outlaws or highwaymen, of course they would come in usefully,' he said to Emily as he climbed into the wagonette. 'It isn't quite such a silly get-up as they usually make me wear. And I've paid out Nanny for curling my crest with the tongs.'

'What have you done?' said Emily in great alarm.

William lifted his hunting cap and showed her that the golden crest which was Nanny's chief pride had disappeared.

'I let Nanny curl it up as much as she chose till it looked like a sausage roll,' he said triumphantly, 'and then I slipped into the night nursery, and cut it off quite close to my head, and put it into an envelope and wrote on it "With William's love", and pinned it on her pillow, and there she will find it when she goes to bed tonight.'

'Oh, William, it was really a very naughty thing to do!' said Emily, much shocked.

'Don't whisper, children,' said Mr Chubb; 'it is a bad habit. You are now going into the very best society, and I must insist that you leave all your vulgar tricks behind you. And that reminds me that I may as well give you a few hints about your manners at table, which often leave much to be desired. Remember, first of all, that you must never ask for a second help.'

'Why?' said William.

'Because it's *not done!*' thundered his father. 'At your age one cannot go into the ins and outs of etiquette, William; you must just accept what you're told and be done with it. Another important rule is that you must not speak till you're spoken to.'

'If everyone kept that rule nobody would ever speak at all,' observed William.

'Don't argue,' said his father. 'Of course the rule only applies to children.'

'How could I tell that? You never said so,' said William in an injured tone.

'William, you bring to my mind the saying that a thankless child is sharper than a serpent's tooth,' said Mr Chubb.

'Have serpents teeth?' asked William, with much interest.

'Of course they . . . William, hold your tongue,' said his father angrily, for he could not feel certain, on second thoughts, whether serpents had teeth or not, and the question recurred to his mind so persistently that he grew quite feverish.

'I hate having these doubts put into my head,' thought poor Mr Chubb. 'Now I shall have no rest until I can look up the question in my *Encyclopædia Britannica.*'

A severe attack of hiccoughs put an end to the possibility of his offering any more excellent advice to his children for the moment.

'This comes of my rushucking about – and doing my packuping – too soon after breakupfast,' gasped poor Mr Chubb.

'A lump of sugar is the best thing,' said Mr Higginbotham timidly, producing some from his pocket. 'I always carry it about with me to drop camphor on in case of a sudden cold.'

Mr Chubb thanked Mr Higginbotham as well as he could, and ate the sugar, but he continued to hiccough as violently as ever.

'I don't believe in sugar,' said Aunt Emily decidedly. 'A sudden fright is far better.'

'Thomas is not easily frightened, Emily,' said Mrs Chubb.

'I suppose even Thomas could be startled by a sudden noise, Maria,' said Aunt Emily pettishly; 'and all I can say is that I believe that, and nothing else, would cure him in a moment.'

As she spoke, William, who was seated next to his father, suddenly blew a loud blast on his horn close to Mr Chubb's ear.

Mr Chubb started in terror, Mrs Chubb screamed, and one of the horses shied so violently up a bank in the narrow lane through which they were passing, that the carriage – already rather top-heavy – was nearly upset, and most of the passengers were thrown out. Almost before Mr Chubb could realise what had happened, he found himself seated on his own hold-all in the hedge; the carriage righted itself miraculously, while the groom flew to the horses' heads and the coachman slowly picked himself out of the ditch into which he, Mr Higginbotham, and Miss Jenkins had all rolled one on the top of another.

Aunt Emily lay on her back in a mud-heap looking at the sky, under the impression that she had been killed suddenly, while sharp little Emily was already busily picking up the various packages which lay scattered over the ground.

Mrs Chubb was nowhere to be found, but by the time the brake with the servants and luggage had arrived on the scene, she was discovered, unhurt but speechless with terror, at the bottom of the wagonette under a heap of rugs.

Having propped up his wife with cushions, and fortified her with a sip of brandy from the flask which Golightly immediately produced from his pocket, Mr Chubb turned his attention to his sister-in-law.

'Were you much hurt, Emily?' he inquired tenderly.

'No, it was quite painless,' said Aunt Emily faintly.

'Then why don't you get up?' said Mr Chubb, sensibly enough.

'Is it time to get up?' said Aunt Emily, surprised to find herself able to speak.

'I am afraid her brain must be injured. It was never strong at the best of times,' said Mr Chubb, looking sorrowfully at Miss Jenkins.

'Let me tell you, Thomas, that my brain is equal to that of any man's on the face of the earth,' said Aunt Emily, scrambling up indignantly.

'We've got all the loose packages in again, sir,' said Golightly. 'The horses are all right, and nobody seems hurt. Had we better get on? The coachman says it's all he'll be able to do to get there by one o'clock at this rate.'

'Certainly get on,' said Mr Chubb, hurrying back to the carriage. 'But where is William? Where is the author of all this mischief? He shall first be made to understand what the weight of my displeasure can be.'

'William is here,' said Mrs Chubb, who was hugging her son closely to her side. 'He has bumped his dear head, and I won't have him scolded, Thomas. I am quite unnerved enough as it is. It was a pure accident. He simply wished to cure your hiccoughs, and had no idea the horses wouldn't like it.'

'Your hiccoughs have entirely ceased, Thomas. I told you so,' said Aunt Emily. 'I knew a good fright was the very thing for you.'

9

THE LUNCHEON-PARTY

They now proceeded on their journey without further mishap, and presently arrived at the lodge gates of the castle.

A picturesque old dame, in a cap and shawl, came out of a model cottage and unfastened the gate for them. She curtseyed so elegantly that Mr Chubb took off his hat and made her a low bow.

'I wish we could persuade the Musbury villagers to behave like this,' he said discontentedly. 'They are terribly off-hand. I must say I am old-fashioned in my ideas, and I like people to be respectful to their betters.'

The wagonette, closely followed by the brake, at length drew

up before the doors of the castle, which were thrown open by a
magnificent butler and by two gigantic footmen who appeared to
be almost falling over backwards with their excess of vicarious
family pride.

Much alarmed at the prospect before her, Mrs Chubb descended
limply from the wagonette, followed by her husband and sister,
her children and her retainers. But inferior servants in the background darted forward to restrain Golightly when he would fain
have shouldered one of his master's trunks, and the brake was
directed to go round with the luggage and servants to a separate
and less imposing entrance.

The haughty butler then turned with a single movement, and
led the way through a large hall filled with statues to a suite of
reception rooms, where he handed his trembling charges over to
the care of a perfectly affable and even kindly personage in black;
and he flung open the door of a lofty saloon and announced their
names to the Duke and Duchess, who were talking to General
Finch at the further end of the apartment.

'For Heaven's sake, Thomas, go first, and let me follow!'
whispered Mrs Chubb, terrified to perceive the expanse of highly
polished oak which she had to traverse before she could reach
the Duchess, who now rose politely to receive her guests.

Mr Chubb hastened forward most willingly, but as the tiger-
skin upon which he stepped was exceedingly slippery, and as he
was not accustomed to highly polished floors, he went much
faster than he intended, for he slid almost the whole length of the
room before he could stop himself, and arrived on all fours at the
very feet of the astonished Duchess.

Warned by his fate, Mrs Chubb and Aunt Emily clung cautiously
to each other, and Miss Jenkins held fast to sharp little Emily's
hand, while Mr Higginbotham had almost a free fight at the
door, in a vain endeavour to walk hand-in-hand with William.

Thus advancing two and two, as though about to dance a
minuet, they all arrived safely at the fireplace.

'What, you here?' said the Duke gloomily, shaking hands with
Mr Higginbotham.

'I'm so glad to see you again, Duke,' said Mr Higginbotham,
who had a very forgiving nature.

'Nonsense!' said the Duke.

This abrupt ejaculation created an awkward pause, which the Duchess hastened to fill up.

'Here is your new cousin, General Finch, William. Aren't you pleased to see him?' she asked.

'I'm pleased to see his *uniform*,' said William truthfully.

'Go and give your new cousin a kiss, William,' said Mrs Chubb reprovingly.

'Men don't kiss each other, Mamma,' said William. 'The General can kiss you and Aunt Emily as much as he likes, and I will kiss the Duchess.'

'So you shall,' said the Duchess, hugging him.

The Admiral and his wife now arrived, followed by Sir Jeremy Wandle, who had also been invited, and they all went in to luncheon.

'Emily,' said Mr Chubb in agitated tones to his sister-in-law, 'are you aware that your back hair is all caked with mud?'

'No, Thomas, I was not; and I think it very unkind of you to tell me,' said Aunt Emily, with spirit. 'Now I shan't be able to enjoy my lunch for thinking of it.'

'It is not noticeable from the sides or the front, so no one at table will be able to perceive it,' said Mr Chubb soothingly.

'But it is not that I care about. What will the servants say? They will all be standing behind me,' said Aunt Emily unhappily. 'You must take the first opportunity of mentioning our accident, Thomas. I don't want the servants to think I go about habitually plastered with mud.'

The Duchess placed William next her on one side, and Sir Jeremy on the other, and Aunt Emily sat by the Admiral, and the General by Mrs Chubb.

Mr Higginbotham was overjoyed to find that his friend John was waiting at table, and could not help whispering to him as he handed the potatoes:

'I am *so* pleased to see you again, John.'

'Hush, sir!' said John angrily.

'Why hush, John? Mayn't I thank you for your kindness to me? I look upon you almost as an old friend.'

'Don't talk,' said John. 'The Duke is looking at you.'

'I'm afraid the Duke doesn't like me, John,' said Mr Higginbotham sadly. 'Can you think why?'

'Yes, I can,' said John, and he took away the dish and hurried to the sideboard, determined not to hand anything more to his old friend.

'You've got through that plate of venison very quickly, William,' said the Duchess kindly. 'Have a little more?'

'No, thank you,' said William, but he could not help sighing.

'Why not?' said the Duchess coaxingly.

'It's *not done*,' said William reproachfully.

'William, how dare you?' said Mr Chubb, in a loud whisper.

'*You* said it wasn't done, Papa,' said William indignantly.

'I don't like venison cooked to a cinder, Mr Chubb,' said the Duke stiffly; 'but if you find the meat at my table raw, you're quite right to say so.'

'But I didn't say so,' said poor Mr Chubb. 'I assure you I haven't even tasted the venison.'

'Then why give an opinion about it at all?' said the Duke.

'Don't contradict him,' whispered the good-natured Duchess. 'He's not accustomed to it, and it always flies to his gouty foot. Do pray try some chicken, Mr Chubb, as you don't fancy the venison.'

Poor Mr Chubb gave up all attempt at further explanation, and turned his attention to the General.

'I am very glad to make your acquaintance, Cousin Benjamin, and I hope you will come and stay with us at Finch Hall.'

'Thank you very much,' said the General. 'I will come as soon as you like. I'm only just back from India, and know very few people in England.'

'I feel rather uncomfortable when I reflect that you have every right to have expected your half-brother to leave his fortune to you instead of to us,' said Mr Chubb.

'Not at all,' said the General politely. 'My half-brother was so much annoyed with me for being born when he was over forty years old, that he never spoke to me in his life, so I expected nothing from him.'

'It's very handsome of you to say that. But if you fancy any of the family treasures, you have only to say so,' said Mr Chubb warmly.

'You are very good, but *the* family treasure was never discovered,' said the General.

'What treasure?'

'Did you never hear the story? There is a legend that a treasure is concealed under the roof of Finch Hall which only a member of the family will find. I fancy he spent a good deal of his time looking for it.'

'Bless me!' cried Mr Chubb. 'We must have a thorough search as soon as we get home. I hope you will come and help us.'

'With pleasure,' said the General.

'We had such a dreadful accident coming here, Duke,' said Mr Higginbotham, whose shrill nasal tones were so penetrating that everyone stopped to listen. 'The carriage fell over on its side, and we all rolled out, and we might have been killed.'

'What of that?' said the Duke, in a voice of thunder.

Poor Mr Higginbotham collapsed in astonishment, and everyone began talking of other things as loudly as they could.

'*Now* the servants will know *why* my back hair is caked with mud,' thought Aunt Emily with great satisfaction.

'How do you like this part of the country, Mrs Chubb?' asked the General, anxious to converse with his newly-found relative.

'I don't like it at all, and I see nothing to like about it,' said Mrs Chubb dismally. 'I much prefer the neighbourhood of the Crystal Palace.'

'You surprise me very much,' said the General. 'I thought Finch Hall was such a beautiful old house. Surely you like living there?'

'Not at all,' said Mrs Chubb. 'It is full of secret staircases behind pictures and all kinds of dreadful things.'

'But it is very large and comfortable.'

'I assure you we were much more comfortable at home,' said poor Mrs Chubb. 'I never know where anyone is, or what they are doing; and there are such quantities of fine servants that it takes half-an-hour or more before I can get so much as a cup of tea. Three men must bring it in at their leisure through miles of corridors, and it is quite bitter and cold by the time it arrives. Now in our old home I could just pop into the kitchen and tell Margery I wanted one, and the kettle was always boiling, and I had it in a moment all fresh and hot.'

'And what have you done with your old house?'

'Mr Chubb's mother is taking care of it. I told Thomas I

would not have it sold. I said if all this fine fortune melted into air one day we might be very glad to get back.'

'And is your sister of the same mind?' asked the General.

'Oh dear, no. Emily and I never think alike. She always disagrees with me, and she has so much spirit that she would order about the servants all day if Thomas allowed her.'

'Quite right, quite right,' said the General warmly, and he looked admiringly across the table at Aunt Emily.

At this moment there was a sudden confusion.

'I am not feeling at all well,' said Mr Higginbotham, looking very pale, 'and I can't help thinking the ice-pudding has disagreed with me.'

'This is the second time within an hour that the food on my table has been found fault with,' said the Duke, glaring at Mr Higginbotham. 'A very little more and I shall lose my temper,' and he began to breathe heavily.

'I find no fault,' said Mr Higginbotham faintly. 'It may be very good for those who like it, but my aunt keeps a plain table, and I am not accustomed to rich food. I should be much obliged if John would assist me to my room, where I have several remedies for violent indigestion in my little bag.'

'John, take him away,' growled the Duke.

'Yes, your Grace,' said John.

As soon as Mr Higginbotham was gone the Duke recovered his temper, and invited his guests to walk round the gardens directly luncheon was over.

'I would rather not,' said Mrs Chubb to the Admiral's wife.

'I am afraid the Duke may be offended if you don't,' whispered Mrs Plumpton. 'He is very peppery.'

'Well, if I must, I must,' said poor Mrs Chubb, 'but it will be very tiring. I wish I had stayed at home.'

Sharp little Emily was all the time engaged in watching her elders, and imitating everything they did, and as coffee and liqueurs and cigarettes were now handed round the table, she copied the Admiral's wife, and took a cup of coffee and a glass of cognac. The latter burnt her throat rather badly, but by taking it alternately with sips of coffee she managed to get it down, and sat in her place smiling for a few moments as though nothing had happened; but the day was warm, Emily was only seven years old, and through the excitement and the fatigue of a long drive and long luncheon was already rather sleepy, so the alcohol presently took effect, and she dropped off into a sound slumber with her head on Sir Jeremy's shoulder and her golden curls dropping over his arm.

'Bless me!' said Sir Jeremy, startled.

'Emily!' said Miss Jenkins, shocked. 'There is a time for everything, and this is not the hour for sleep.'

But Emily slept on serenely.

'Poor little thing, was she so very tired?' the Duchess asked William.

'I expect the brandy got into her head,' said William placidly. 'I thought it would when I saw her drink it.'

'Then why didn't you warn us what she was doing, sir?' asked his father.

'You told me not to speak unless I was spoken to,' said William indignantly.

'Georgiana, have you five shillings about you?' asked the Admiral in a low voice, for he realised suddenly that he had not yet tipped William.

'Yes, Admiral, I have, and I shall require it to pay our cab home,' said his wife sternly.

'Well, well, it must be for another time,' said the Admiral, disappointed.

As it was found to be impossible to wake Emily, John, who had now returned, was directed to carry her into an adjoining room, where she was to be laid on a sofa, and Miss Jenkins was requested to watch by her until she woke up again.

'I have enough to do, carrying them all out of the room one after another. I never did see such a party,' muttered John to himself, but he carried Emily away very carefully.

'I shall be very glad to sit and watch over her,' said Miss Jenkins, 'and if only she wakes in time I will try and get in half-an-hour's dictation before tea. Emily's spelling is disgraceful!' Miss Jenkins then followed John out of the room, and the rest of the party made ready to accompany the Duke round the castle grounds.

10

THE AFTERNOON WALK

In the kitchen garden the Duchess invited her guests to take what fruit they chose, and the Duke, who was the soul of kindness when nothing happened to annoy him, gathered some ripe figs for Mrs Chubb and Aunt Emily with his own hands, and showed William the way into the wire cage which contained the currant and raspberry bushes.

'This is what I call *true* hospitality,' said Aunt Emily. 'If you will believe me, General, we are not allowed to gather so much as a single plum for ourselves at Finch Hall; the gardener guards the fruit like a dragon.'

The General, who had watched Aunt Emily eat seven figs and five apricots, with some alarm for the consequences, was relieved to find that she seemed none the worse for her feast, but he could not help thinking it was perhaps fortunate that the gardener at Finch Hall *did* guard the fruit like a dragon.

'Fruit, in moderation, is excellent,' he said cautiously.

'It is the most wholesome thing in the world,' said Aunt Emily. 'And I am going to take that delicious ripe greengage off the wall this very moment.'

'Allow me,' said the General, putting up his eyeglass.

'No, no. It is half the fun to gather it for oneself,' said Aunt Emily; and with surprising agility she stepped lightly over the carnation bed towards the object of her desires. As she did so she heard a slight click, felt something graze her ankle, and found the hem of her best lavender silk dress held fast.

'What has happened?' said Aunt Emily faintly, as she strove in vain to release herself.

'You seem to be caught in some kind of trap,' said the General, alarmed. 'I trust you are not hurt.'

'I am not so much hurt as I might have been,' said Aunt Emily indignantly; 'but I must say I think it a very cruel thing for the Duke to invite visitors to gather fruit for themselves, and then set traps for them like so many mice.'

The Duke now hastened up, fearing something was wrong, as Aunt Emily remained motionless in the carnation bed, stretching out her arms like a scarecrow, while the General knelt at her feet, endeavouring in vain to open the trap.

'It seems to be half buried in the earth,' he said, red with exertion.

'It *is* buried in the earth,' said the Duke. 'It is my new patent mole-trap. How very unfortunate! It can only be unlocked with a key, and Timothy Tighe has that.'

'Then pray let Timothy Tighe be sent for at once,' said Aunt Emily tartly.

'We had better go and fetch him ourselves,' said the Duchess, looking at the Duke. 'He is rather easily offended. But I am afraid it will take some time to get him, for he lives at the south lodge, with his wife.'

'Wouldn't it be better if you let me cut a little bit out of your skirt?' said the Admiral's wife, producing a pair of scissors from her châtelaine. 'It could be mended not to show, and it will be so tiring for you to stand here.'

'Nothing would induce me to sacrifice any portion of this valuable silk,' said Aunt Emily firmly. 'I have not so many fine dresses that I can afford to cut them to pieces every time I get caught in a trap. If I am tired of standing I can very easily sit down.'

'I *hope* you won't sit down on my picotees,' said the Duchess pleadingly. 'I am *so* fond of them.'

'Permit me to bring you a seat,' said the General, and he brought a large flower-pot and turned it upside down, and Aunt Emily sat upon it.

'Could you slip off your skirt, Emily, when we are all gone, and run home in your petticoat?' whispered Mr Chubb.

'Certainly not, Thomas,' said Aunt Emily, scandalised. 'What would the servants say?'

'Bother the servants!' said Mr Chubb.

'We had better go to the lodge without delay,' said the Duke, and they hurried off, leaving Aunt Emily alone with the General, who gallantly refused to desert her.

The Duke paused for a moment to point out his gooseberry bushes to Mr Chubb, saying:

'Look here! Did you ever see anything like it?'

'Charming, charming!' said Mr Chubb, who was determined to admire everything he saw, even gooseberry bushes.

'I don't know what you mean by charming,' said the Duke crossly. 'I am showing you the new American blight. It's a peculiarly fatal kind, and every one of these bushes will have to be grubbed up by the roots and burnt.'

'You don't say so,' said poor Mr Chubb.

They now left the gardens and proceeded through the park to the lodge, followed by a herd of cattle, which was annoyed by the yapping of the Duchess's little dog. Mrs Chubb clung tightly to the Admiral's arm, for she was not only excessively fatigued, but also very much afraid of cows.

'Timothy Tighe and his wife are great favourites of ours,' said the Duchess. 'They have been in the service of the family for over fifty years. He was a ploughman, and she was a housemaid at the castle.'

'How very interesting,' said Mrs Chubb faintly.

'We feel they have a claim upon us, so we put them into one of the lodges rent-free, and pay the old woman for opening the gates and the old man for setting traps in the garden. Of course, he's not allowed to set any *outside* the garden.'

'I'm glad of that,' said Mrs Chubb, who had been almost afraid to put her foot to the ground since Aunt Emily's mishap.

'Because *that* would interfere with our regular mole-catcher,' said the Duchess. 'But they insist on having work given them. They *won't* live on charity, and they are a pattern couple, setting an example to the whole village by their respect, ability and sobriety.'

'They cost me a pretty penny, one way and another,' growled the Duke.

'Yes, it was a pity they insisted on having the lodge rebuilt,' said the Duchess, sighing. 'It was so *very* picturesque. Some of Cromwell's soldiers are said to have lodged there.'

'William, do you hear that?' said his father, determined that his son should display his intelligent interest in the conversation.

'Hear what?' said William.

'That Cromwell's soldiers used to lodge there?'

'Lodge where?' said William.

'In the lodge, of course. I mean not in the lodge, but in what used to be the lodge before the lodge was built,' said Mr Chubb, trying to explain.

'It used *not* to be the *lodge*,' said the Duchess; 'it was a look-out tower. The old well remains, and the bucket they are supposed to have used.'

'I'd like to see *that*,' said William.

'William, I desire you won't go near it,' said his mother, in a great fright.

'I'll take care he doesn't fall in,' said the Duke. 'Leave it to me.'

'You don't know how heedless boys can be, Duke,' said Mr Chubb, shaking his head.

They now arrived at the lodge, and the same old woman who had opened the gates to them in the morning appeared in the doorway and curtseyed, while her husband, in a spotless smock-frock of the olden time, touched his forelock respectfully.

'*I* make him those smock-frocks,' whispered the Duchess, 'and he won't wear them unless I stitch a bit of blue ribbon in the front opening. Isn't it touching?'

The Duke now took William round to the back of the lodge to show him Cromwell's well, and, determined he should have no chance of falling in, he held him tightly by the hand and took him behind the stone parapet which surrounded it on three sides, while Mr Chubb guarded the steps of the opening.

'This is the way to work the windlass, William,' said the Duke, showing him how to wind and unwind the chain to which the bucket was fastened. 'I will now drop in a pebble, and you can estimate the depth of the well by the time which it takes to reach the water. Listen, and you will hear a little splash.'

Mr Chubb leant forward eagerly and listened to the little splash, but the steps on which he stood were so slippery that he unfortunately lost his balance, and before the Duke could stretch out a hand to save him, a much louder splash announced that his guest was in a position to estimate for himself the time it took to reach the water.

William, with much presence of mind, seized the winch, and with the assistance of the Duke let down the bucket, and then ran for help, while the Duke leant over the parapet and shouted encouragement to poor Mr Chubb.

'How are you?'

'I am in the well!' said a faint voice far below.

'I know that,' shouted the Duke. 'What I mean is, can you hold on to the bucket chain for a moment while we fetch a rope? I am afraid the chain would not be strong enough to bear your weight.'

'Yes,' said Mr Chubb. 'But be quick; the water is like ice.'

The Admiral now hurried round the corner of the cottage with a fine new rope which Timothy Tighe fortunately had on the premises; and the rest of the party, full of agitation and alarm, crowded round the mouth of the well, where the Duchess in vain endeavoured to console Mrs Chubb by assuring her that if Mr Chubb were drowned she knew how to restore him.

'Keep up his spirits!' cried the Admiral. 'I shan't be a moment,' and the gallant old sailor knotted some loops, made fast one end of the rope to a plum tree and lowered the other cautiously down the well, his wife clinging to his waist all the time, for fear he should overbalance himself and fall in.

'Slip it over your shoulders and under your arms, not round your neck, or you will be hanged!' he shouted encouragingly. 'Call out when you are ready, and we'll haul you up, very slowly.'

A faint hallo announced that Mr Chubb was ready to be pulled up, and the Admiral, the Duke and the Mayor, old Tighe and little William hauled with all their might, aided by the ladies. Mr Chubb's head presently appeared over the edge of the well, and his wife was so overjoyed to see it that she immediately let go the rope and fainted; but the others, being less overcome by their emotion, were enabled to pull Mr Chubb out and lift him carefully onto the grass, where the rope was taken off him.

'I'm afraid you've no brandy in the house, Mrs Tighe,' said the Duchess anxiously.

'Oh, your Grace!' said Mrs Tighe reproachfully. 'I'll do what's far better than giving him brandy. Pop my warming-pan into my spare bed, and let the poor gentleman take off his wet clothes and get in between the blankets, and I'll make him some hot gruel.'

A few moments later Mr Chubb was lying warm and snug in Mrs Tighe's spare bed, while his wet clothes were taken into the back kitchen to have the water wrung out of them.

'How do you feel now?' said the Duke anxiously.

'I feel very well, thank you,' said Mr Chubb, 'though distressed to have given so much trouble.'

'I'll tell you what I'll do,' said the Duke. 'I'll go back to the house and send down my servant with a suit of dry clothes and some whisky. A stiff tumbler of hot grog would be the best thing you could take.'

'Thank you,' said Mr Chubb, 'but I should fear to shock my worthy hosts; and I would prefer to take the grog upon my return to your hospitable roof, and be contented for the present with gruel. But I have no need to borrow your clothes, for my own servant can come down with my things. I brought several suits with me, not knowing how many I might require.'

'Bless me!' said the Duke, much astonished at such extraordinary forethought.

Mrs Chubb entreated to be allowed to remain with her husband, but Mr Chubb would not hear of it.

'We must not forget, my love, that all this time poor Emily is sitting on a flower-pot in the sun, and that the General may be growing very tired of her conversation, as I sometimes do myself,' he said reproachfully. 'Do not, Maria, let your very natural excitement and pleasure in this visit make you neglectful of your only sister.'

'So far as we have gone, there has been plenty of excitement but very little pleasure, Thomas,' said his wife dejectedly. 'But I will do whatever you wish.'

The whole party, with the exception of Mr Chubb, then returned to the kitchen garden, taking the key, with instructions from Timothy Tighe as to the manner of using it.

'Why can't he come and unlock it himself?' said the Duke.

'My dear, it's his tea time,' said the Duchess reproachfully.

' 'Ave they gone, Sarah Ann?' asked Timothy Tighe, when his dame had stood curtseying in the doorway for some five minutes.

'They 'ave, Timothy,' said Mrs Tighe, with a sigh of relief.

'And are you sure him as is upstairs won't come down?' asked Mr Tighe, jerking his thumb towards the staircase.

'He can't come down, for he ain't got nothing to come down in; and besides, he's had his gruel, and is dropping off to sleep,' said Sarah Ann.

'Then gimme my pipe and a drop of beer,' said Timothy Tighe, and the worthy couple comforted themselves with a little refreshment after their past exertions.

Blissfully unconscious of the Tighes' duplicity, the Duke and Duchess now proceeded to release Aunt Emily, who was much concerned to learn of the accident which had befallen her brother-in-law. They then hurried on to the castle to send some dry clothes to Mr Chubb, and here an upper servant advanced very gravely and spoke to the Duchess in a low tone.

The Duchess, whose face assumed a very agitated expression during his communication, in her turn called the Duke aside and whispered to him, after begging her guests to proceed to the drawing-room, where tea was awaiting them.

'I don't understand you, Sophia,' said the Duke angrily. 'How can they have come to stay, when they were only invited to lunch?'

'They must have misread my letter,' said the Duchess.

'This comes of your villainous handwriting,' said the Duke, frowning. 'How long do they propose to stay?'

'I can't tell you at all, Charlemagne,' said the Duchess helplessly. 'I suppose we can't send them away, can we?'

'Of course we can't send them away. A Pontypool cannot lay himself open to the charge of inhospitality,' said the Duke haughtily. 'There is nothing for it but to put up with them. I only insist upon one thing. That tutor must not be allowed to come near me. He gets on my nerves.'

'So he does on mine, but one can't be rude to him, you know,' said the Duchess sadly. 'They *all* get on my nerves, except William.'

As there was nothing else to be done, the Duke and Duchess resolved to put a good face on the matter, and, returning to the drawing-room, sent a polite message to invite Miss Jenkins and Emily to come to tea.

Emily was now quite rested and refreshed by her long slumber, and was led in by Miss Jenkins looking very pretty in her quaint Dutch frock with her golden curls falling round her fair, pointed little face. The Admiral, who was fond of children, lifted her on to his knee and gave her cakes and bonbons, and petted and praised her to her heart's content, while the Duchess saw that William had everything he wanted, so that both children enjoyed themselves very much.

The Duke, who was nearly as tired as Mrs Chubb with the long afternoon walk and the various annoyances of the day, was very glad to rest in his armchair and refresh himself with a cup of tea; and so was Sir Jeremy Wandle, who, being rather stout and not very young, was quite as much fatigued as the Duke. The afternoon was hot, and the air came pleasantly into the luxuriously shaded room through the long windows opening onto the lawn. The table round which they sat was also pleasant to look upon, with its snowy embroidered cloth, massive gilt tea equipage, dainty dishes of cakes and fruit, frosted silver jugs of fresh cream, and crystal pitchers of iced coffee and lemonade. The Duchess wore an exquisite cool gown of pale blue chiffon, with a turquoise-studded belt and a large black hat, and looked so handsome that William and Emily could hardly take their eyes off her.

Mrs Chubb felt the soothing influence of the scene so much

that only by drinking cup after cup of the strongest China tea
could she keep herself from nodding, and Aunt Emily was just
informing the General that she had never in her life felt so happy
or at home anywhere on the face of the earth, when the door
opened and a nasal voice inquired:

'May I come in?'

The voice was followed by Mr Higginbotham, who came smiling into the room.

'I feel so *much* better,' he said. 'I took half a teaspoonful of
bicarbonate of soda, and it has made me quite a different man.'

The Duke's face became as black as thunder, but the Duchess
looked entreatingly at him, and he said nothing.

'How silent you all are!' said Mr Higginbotham, in wonder. 'I
do hope there hasn't been . . .'

'Sit down, take your tea, and hold your tongue, Mr Higginbotham,' said Miss Jenkins in a stern whisper.

Mr Higginbotham was too much surprised to expostulate. He
sat down, spread his handkerchief on his knee, and made a substantial meal; while the Admiral, the General, and Sir Jeremy all
talked of the weather and the crops as loudly as they could in
order to cheer up the Duke.

Mr Chubb now arrived, looking none the worse for his accident,
and loud in his praises of Timothy Tighe and his wife.

'They spoke of your Grace's kindness with tears in their eyes,'
said Mr Chubb warmly. 'They said since a bathroom had been
added to their humble home they had nothing left to wish for –
except a hot-air linen cupboard.'

'They've bothered me about that hot-air linen cupboard a
dozen times,' growled the Duke.

'I think we *ought* to give it to them, Charlemagne,' said the
Duchess. 'Mrs Tighe says she's getting very old to carry a heavy
brass warming-pan up and down stairs.'

'That reminds me. They begged me to speak to you about the
widening of their staircase, which they said her Grace had very
kindly promised,' began Mr Chubb, when a loud scream from
Mr Higginbotham interrupted him.

A wasp which had been hovering over the jam sandwich he was
devouring had settled upon his nose just as the last crumb disappeared into his capacious mouth. Mr Higginbotham had en-

deavoured to brush it off under the impression that it was a harmless bluebottle, and the wasp had immediately and severely stung him.

'If it were anywhere else I should not mind nearly so much,' sobbed Mr Higginbotham, dancing with the smart, 'but the tip of my nose is particularly tender. I always get a chilblain there in winter, and now to get a wasp's sting in summer seems almost too much.'

'Blue is the only safe remedy,' said the Duchess, ringing the bell. 'John, send at once to the laundry for the blue-bag.'

'What a very unfortunate occurrence,' said the Duke, but his tone was suspiciously cheerful.

'I don't feel as if anybody really cared,' whispered Mr Higginbotham dolefully to Miss Jenkins. 'When I think of what my aunt's feelings would have been I can hardly understand your composure. Take care!' he added, with a shriek; 'it is crawling on your shoulder now.'

Miss Jenkins merely clapped her hand smartly upon the insect and threw it out of the window.

'It is quite harmless now,' she said calmly. 'The sting is in your nose.'

The blue-bag was brought, and the Duchess, always interested in healing, dipped it into water and covered Mr Higginbotham's nose, which was by this time terribly swollen, with blue; and very odd he looked when she had finished with him.

'You had better go back to your room and lie down, Mr Higginbotham,' she said kindly. 'I will have your dinner sent up to you. And above all, don't wash off the blue, or the pain will return.'

'Thank you very much,' said Mr Higginbotham, 'but be sure I shall make every effort to come down. I would not spoil everybody's pleasure by stopping away for anything.'

II

THE NOCTURNAL ADVENTURE

The carriage which was to convey the Admiral and his wife, Sir Jeremy, and the General to the station (for they had all come by train from Burridge) was now announced, and the Duchess having taken leave of her guests, offered to show Mrs Chubb her room.

'I shall be very grateful indeed,' said poor Mrs Chubb, who was almost worn out with the events of the day, and she and Aunt Emily, followed by William and his sister and Miss Jenkins, all trooped upstairs with the kind Duchess.

Mr Chubb then privately asked John to show him the way to the library, for he had been turning over the question of serpents'

teeth in his own mind until he felt positively giddy, and felt he
should get no sleep at night unless he could once for all put his
doubts on the subject to rest.

John indicated the door of the library to him in the most
affable manner; and the Duke, delighted to be free from his self-
invited guests, if only for a moment, hurried upstairs to his own
sanctum, which was a pleasant apartment on the first floor, opening into his dressing-room, and situated over an archway which
led to an immense courtyard next the stables.

Mr Chubb saw the Duke depart with almost equal relief, and
went happily into the library, shutting the door behind him.

He found himself in a large room, not very well lighted, and
lined from floor to ceiling with books. Perceiving an encyclopædia
before him, he tried to take it down, and found to his annoyance
that it was a dummy. Much disappointed, he looked for another
encyclopædia, but his search was vain. Fearing to be late for
dinner, he then turned to leave the room, but the door being made
of bookshelves to match the walls, he was unable to find it, and,
covered with confusion, was presently obliged to ring for a servant
to show him the way out of the apartment he had been so anxious
to enter.

Meantime Mr Higginbotham had hastened upstairs, intending
to return to his bedroom, but the castle was very large, and built
on three sides of a square, and as he turned to the right instead of
to the left on reaching the top of the grand staircase, he found
himself in the opposite wing to that in which his own room was
situated.

'John said I was to count seven pillars, and I know there was a
little archway and two steps to go down,' said Mr Higginbotham,
proceeding cautiously along the corridor. 'One, two, three, four,
five, six, seven. *Here* I am.'

He opened the door triumphantly and entered a small, comfortable study.

'Dear me, this is not the room. They can't have taken away my
bed – and my little bag,' thought poor Mr Higginbotham. 'What
shall I do? I'll look out of the window and see if the view is the
same as from my room, and if it is not I shall know I must have
come to the wrong side of the house.'

The windows were wide open, and Mr Higginbotham had just

crossed the room on tiptoe to look out, when the Duke, whose private den he had invaded, suddenly came out of the adjoining dressing-room in a smoking-jacket, carrying the revolver which he always kept by his bedside, and which he examined every evening to make sure that it was in good order.

On catching sight of the intruder, he flew into a fury which terrified poor Mr Higginbotham out of his senses.

'How dare you come here, sir?' shouted the Duke. 'Is no corner of my house to remain unpolluted by your presence? Leave the room instantly – *instantly!*'

The Duke forgot entirely that he had a loaded pistol in his hand, and gesticulated so violently that the revolver went off unexpectedly, frightening Mr Higginbotham so much that, without knowing what he was doing, he jumped out of the window to escape, thus leaving the room yet more suddenly than his host had anticipated.

The Duke was naturally much upset when he realised what had happened, for, being at heart a most humane man, he had no wish to injure anyone, and his first impulse was to run to the window and look out after Mr Higginbotham; but as he was really almost too agitated to move, and as his doctor had ordered him to avoid shocks, second thoughts prevailed, and he sank into a chair and pressed the electric bell attached to his writing-table.

John came in a moment, for it was well understood in the household that it was better not to keep his Grace waiting.

'John,' said the Duke, 'look out of the window and tell me what you see.'

John, much astonished, looked out of the window.

'I see nothing particular, your Grace. Everything is just as usual.'

'Look again. Look down, John, at the ground beneath the window.'

Fearing the Duke had gone suddenly mad, John leant out as far as he could, and stared at the gravel road beneath the window.

'Nothing at all, your Grace.'

The Duke began to think he must have been dreaming.

'Possibly the whole thing was an hallucination,' he reflected. 'How do I look, John?' he said aloud.

'If your Grace will excuse me – rather wild-like,' said John, hesitating.

'Go and run right round the house, John, and look inside the archway under my window and round the courtyard as quickly as you can, and come back and tell me if you see or hear anything strange,' said the Duke. 'If you don't I shall know I am not very well.'

John was now sure that the Duke had taken leave of his senses, but being a faithful servant, he did exactly as he was told; and as he was returning breathless from his fruitless mission, he met the Duke's medical attendant, who lived in the castle, and advised him to go up and see his Grace immediately.

'I always feared this pernicious habit of giving way to his temper would affect the Duke's brain sooner or later,' thought the doctor, and he ran upstairs with John at once.

'Good evening, your Grace,' said the doctor, but the Duke was so busy following out his own train of thought that he took no notice.

'How are you feeling this evening, your Grace?' said the doctor in a louder tone.

'Has there been much rain lately?' asked the Duke, for, being slightly confused with shock and anxiety combined, it occurred to him as possible that the ground might be soft, and that Mr Higginbotham had fallen through it, thus, as it were, killing and burying himself at one blow.

This question from the Duke, who tapped his barometer every morning of his life, convinced the doctor that something must be wrong.

'Has his Grace been wandering at all?' he asked John.

'No, sir,' said John, much agitated. 'His Grace has been sitting perfectly still where you see him now.'

'In my position, the first thing is to avoid scandal,' said the Duke.

'Quite so, quite so,' said the doctor soothingly. 'But if I give you a couple of small pills they will clear everything unpleasant away in a moment, and no one need be any the wiser.'

'Then you think it *was* a dream?' said the Duke.

'I am certain of it,' said the doctor.

'And yet I feel sure it really happened,' said the Duke, with a puzzled look.

'You are not in a fit state to judge,' said the doctor, shaking his head compassionately. 'Whatever it may have been, however, it has evidently passed off. You are quite yourself again at this moment.'

'Then would you advise me to go down to dinner as though nothing unusual had occurred?' said the Duke.

'As your medical adviser I order you to do so,' said the doctor. 'Pleasant company is the very thing to distract you, and so long as I am there to watch over you there can be no danger.'

By this time, had the Duke but known it, Mr Higginbotham was nearly half a mile away from the castle, for by great good luck he had fallen plump into the wagon-load of straw which was being carried from the stables to the farmyard on the other side of the park.

Though unhurt, he was too much alarmed to move for some time, but at last he looked cautiously out of his resting-place, saw the carter's head immediately beneath him, and divined what had happened.

The carter being young, in love, and light-hearted, was whistling a merry tune to himself.

'Hallo!' said Mr Higginbotham.

The carter stopped whistling and stared round him wildly.

'Don't be frightened,' said Mr Higginbotham.

'I ain't no call to be frightened,' said the carter in a trembling voice. 'My conscience is clear. Who's speaking?'

'Look up and you will see,' said Mr Higginbotham.

The carter shuddered and looked up. When he saw Mr Higginbotham's immense bright blue nose, he gave a yell, jumped off the driving seat, and ran up the road to the nearest cottage as fast as he could.

The horses came to a standstill, and Mr Higginbotham climbed cautiously down from his perch, feeling the best thing he could do was to walk back to the castle, which was visible in the distance.

He arrived at the principal entrance just as John was superintending the shutting, bolting, and barring of the great front doors for the night.

'I thought you were safe in your room, sir,' said John, much annoyed at beholding him.

'I've had such a dreadful accident, John,' said Mr Higginbotham breathlessly. 'The Duke shot me out of the window on to a wagon full of straw with his little pistol.'

Faithful John now began to understand the Duke's strange behaviour.

'Well, sir, I don't blame him,' he said staunchly. 'What was you a-doing in his Grace's room?'

'I lost the way to my own room, John, and got into his by mistake,' said Mr Higginbotham. 'It was an accident that might have happened to anybody, but the Duke doesn't like me – I can't think why, for I have taken every opportunity of speaking civilly to *him* – so he resented it.'

'Well, I don't wonder,' said John. 'If you'll excuse me for saying so, you talk much too familiar to his Grace for a perfect stranger, and it's a great liberty on your part, sir.'

'I know you're a true friend, John,' said Mr Higginbotham, weeping, 'so you can say what you like to me.'

'Don't cry before the servants, sir, for pity's sake,' said John. 'If you must cry, come upstairs and have a good cry in your own bedroom and be done with it. As it is, you're simply washing the blue off your nose and on to the carpet.'

For fear of any more mistakes, he then led Mr Higginbotham up to his bedroom.

'Won't you help me to dress for dinner?' said Mr Higginbotham, clinging to him.

'No, sir, I won't,' said John. 'I've got orders to bring your dinner up here on a tray, and though it goes against the grain for me to be carrying trays up and down stairs, I'm going to do it. How can you sit at table with a nose like that? The under-footmen, who isn't used to control theirselves as we are, might be led to forget their places and burst out laughing. It's enough to make even a butler smile; and then what would happen?'

And to make sure that Mr Higginbotham could not come down, he prudently assisted him to bed, and carried away all his clothes on pretence of brushing them.

John then went to the Duke and recounted what he knew of Mr Higginbotham's adventure, and the Duke was so much relieved that he raised the faithful creature's wages on the spot, and went down to dinner in the best of spirits.

Miss Jenkins sent a message that she would prefer to have her supper upstairs with William and Emily, so that quite a small party sat down to table eventually; and after dinner the Duchess,

Aunt Emily, the doctor, and Mr Chubb played bridge, while Mrs Chubb dozed in one corner of the saloon and the Duke in the other; and except for a few rather heated arguments between Aunt Emily and Mr Chubb, the evening passed off very well.

At half-past ten everyone went to bed, and very glad Mrs Chubb was to be allowed to retire so early. She was so much fatigued that she went to sleep almost the moment her head touched the pillow, but Mr Chubb, tormented by his uncertainty regarding serpents' teeth, lay awake and argued out the question with himself for at least an hour and a half.

Just as he was gliding into a gentle doze, however, he was unpleasantly disturbed by a splash of cold water on his face. His first impression was that it had been raining, and he groped feebly for his umbrella; but a second heavier splash brought him to his senses, and he remembered where he was, lit a candle, and sat up in alarm.

'What can be the matter, Thomas?' asked his wife sleepily.

'The matter is that the water is pouring through the ceiling and descending in a perfect shower upon the bed,' said Mr Chubb. 'Rise at once, Maria, and don your wrapper. It is clear that either a pipe or a cistern in the roof has burst. I must disturb the household and give the alarm instantly, or incalculable damage may be done.'

Without losing a moment Mr Chubb slipped on his dressing-gown – which was a brand new one of a beautiful flowered pattern – and hurried down the passage to the door of the Duke's room. As he ran, he became conscious of a smell of burning, which redoubled his anxiety to disturb the household, and he banged on the Duke's door with all his might.

'Who is there?' shouted a furious voice.

'It is I, Thomas Chubb. Come to the door at once,' replied his visitor.

'Am I to have no peace day or night, Sophia?' demanded the Duke angrily. 'Understand me, once for all, either the Chubbs or I leave this house tomorrow.'

'Do, pray, see what the matter is, Charlemagne,' said the Duchess, trembling.

'Whatever it may be, they must and shall be made to understand that my own apartments are sacred,' grumbled the Duke, dressing himself as fast as he could in the dark.

Mrs Chubb now appeared in her old scarlet dressing-gown, with her hair screwed up in curl-papers, and cried down the corridor to her husband that she too was aware of the smell of burning. Mr Chubb then determined to hasten the Duke's movements, so he thumped at his door again, and shouted 'Fire!' as loudly as he could.

'Where?' cried the Duke, dashing out of his room in a great hurry.

'I can't see it, but I smell it,' said Mr Chubb excitedly. 'I came to tell you at the same time that one of your water-pipes must have burst, for the water is pouring through the ceiling of my room. I do not know if we happen to be sleeping under a cistern.'

'Sleeping under a cistern, nonsense!' said the Duchess; 'you are under the nurseries. I put dear little William and Emily in the rooms over yours.'

'Then depend upon it dear little William and Emily are responsible for whatever has happened,' retorted the Duke savagely, and he rang the alarm bell which hung in the corridor, with all his might.

Instantly servants in every conceivable variety of attire came running along the passages and down the stairs, while Mr and Mrs Chubb in agony flew to the rescue of their beloved little ones, followed by their host and hostess and several members of the household, who traced the smell of burning to the nurseries.

A scene of confusion met their eyes as they opened the door of little Emily's bedroom, which communicated with that of William.

Water was dripping from the bed into a large pool on the carpet, wherein Emily's little slippers were floating.

The bedclothes, blackened and scorched, and soaked through and through, lay in a heap on the mattress, and Emily herself was nowhere to be seen.

Mrs Chubb, believing her child had been reduced to ashes, rushed in terror to the adjoining room, and there beheld Emily sleeping serenely in William's bed, while William lay rolled in a blanket upon the sofa.

Too much relieved to care for anything but the fact that both her children were safe and sound, Mrs Chubb woke Emily by kissing and hugging her, while Mr Chubb demanded an explanation from the startled William.

'It was my fault, Mamma,' said Emily, as soon as she was sufficiently awake to understand the questions poured out by the throng who now pressed into the children's bedroom. 'I was so pleased by what the Admiral said about my curls that I begged Molly to frizz them with her own hair-tongs after Miss Jenkins had said goodnight, so Molly came back when she had had her supper and waved my hair; and it took a long time, and when she had finished she must have put the hot tongs down on the bed and left them there, for I smelt something singeing before I went to sleep. And the next thing I remember was waking up and seeing flames; and then William pulled me out of bed, and we poured the bath over it to put out the fire; and William put me in his warm bed and went to sleep on the sofa himself.'

Mrs Chubb dropped Emily and seized William, whom she kissed and wept over in turn. 'He has saved his sister's life,' she sobbed.

'Very likely he has,' said his father testily. 'But why couldn't he go and get help instead of going to sleep; then the water could have been mopped up, and the ceiling of our room wouldn't have been spoilt.'

'Nonsense!' said the Duchess warmly. 'Dear little William has probably saved the house from being burnt down. What is a paltry ceiling in comparison?'

'It is an Adams ceiling,' muttered the Duke.

'Miss Jenkins took away the matches,' said William, 'and I was afraid of going to fetch her or Molly, for in the dark I might have gone into the wrong room, and Mr Higginbotham came down specially to warn me of the danger of doing that.'

'Humph,' said the Duke uncomfortably.

'Well, well, I will not deny you showed great presence of mind, William,' said his father. 'And I must insist on being allowed to repair any damage, Duke, that has been done by my son's gallant but thoughtless behaviour; for since I am now in a position which makes expense no consideration whatever . . .'

'Nonsense, Mr Chubb, nonsense!' said the Duke. 'We are all too much beholden to William to hear of any such thing.'

'All this can be discussed in the morning,' said the Duchess, shivering. 'The sooner we get back to bed now the better.'

'I couldn't bear to lose sight of the children again,' said Mrs Chubb, 'so I shall stay where I am; and as our bed is quite as wet as Emily's, Thomas had better spend the rest of the night in his dressing-room.'

The servants had by this time mopped up as much water as possible in Emily's room, and placed vessels in the room below to catch the remainder, so the Duke and Duchess retired thankfully to bed, and Mr and Mrs Chubb were left to rejoice over their offspring's safety undisturbed.

'All's well that ends well, Maria,' said Mr Chubb. 'The only thing that disturbs me is that you should have cut such an odd figure before the servants in that old red dressing-gown. Considering that expense is now no object, I cannot understand why you have not got a beautiful quilted silk garment like the Duchess.'

'I *have* got one, Thomas, and I brought it with me; it is hanging in my wardrobe now. And the servants are quite welcome to go and look at it if they choose,' said Mrs Chubb; 'but I prefer to go on wearing this all the same. It is full of old associations which a new one, however expensive, would lack. Every patch and darn which ornaments it recalls some precious memory of Dorothea's teething or Charles's whooping-cough, when I used to sit up in it all night; and though it has certainly shrunk through being cleaned so often, and even lost its colour here and there, it is still warm and comfortable.'

'It may be so, Maria, but it is not becoming,' said Mr Chubb. 'However, after tonight you may wear it as much as you choose, for I have decided that the strain of keeping up my spirits through all the anxiety caused by mishaps in other people's houses is too great, and therefore I am determined to invent an excuse for going home early tomorrow morning.'

'I am very glad to hear it, Thomas,' said his wife thankfully. 'And I do not think an excuse will be necessary, for the Duke told me at dinner that he and the Duchess were going up to Scotland tomorrow, though I did not like to tell you so earlier, for fear of spoiling your night's rest with the disappointment.'

12

THE BEANFEAST

'I have been thinking, my love,' said Mr Chubb to his wife as soon as they were once more safely settled at Finch Hall, 'that we ought to give some kind of a beanfeast to our neighbours.'

'I don't know what you mean by a beanfeast, but I will do just as you wish, Thomas,' said Mrs Chubb.

'I should like to combine a garden-party with a school-treat,' explained Mr Chubb. 'We don't know enough people yet to give a garden-party, and there are too few residents in this very small village for a regular fête, so it struck me as an excellent idea to combine the two.'

'You are always full of ideas, Thomas. I can't tell where you get them from, I'm sure,' said his wife admiringly.

'I suppose they come naturally to me,' said Mr Chubb modestly. 'What do *you* think, Emily? Is it not an excellent plan for entertaining rich and poor at one blow, so to speak?'

'If you ask my opinion, Thomas, I think you will succeed in offending everyone all round, and you had much better give nothing at all than mix up people in such a higgledy-piggledy fashion,' said Aunt Emily.

'You always take a gloomy view, Emily,' said Mr Chubb.

'I say what I think, Thomas,' said Aunt Emily. 'When I agreed to share your home you will recollect it was on condition I should preserve my independence.'

'It will give the children something to think of, Emily,' said Mrs Chubb, 'for they must miss the Crystal Palace very much.'

'My dear, you are always harping on the Crystal Palace,' said Mr Chubb.

'Well, Thomas, it was a great resource, especially in bad weather, and as we had season tickets, Emily and I used to enjoy sitting there with our knitting on half-holidays, and listening to the music, while the children wandered about and amused themselves.'

'I am sure I should enjoy a beanfeast better still,' said Greedy George, with glistening eyes.

'Well, as I wish you all to acquire a sense of responsibility,' said his father, 'I shall allow you to help to entertain our guests when they come. There must be sports, of course, and competitions of all kinds, from croquet to egg-and-spoon races; and since expense is no object, I shall send for some really beautiful prizes, which your Mamma will give away; and I shall make a short speech from time to time, whenever it seems to be required. I am sure our friend the Admiral will assist us, and Sir Jeremy Wandle, who is the soul of good-nature; and I have every hope that your Cousin Benjamin, General Finch, will be staying with us on the occasion – in fact, we must endeavour to select a date to suit him.'

The General was very much pleased to accept the invitation of his new cousins, and the day selected for the proposed entertainment proved to be as fine as could be desired.

At about four o'clock most of the guests had arrived. Mr and

Mrs Chubb and Aunt Emily, all very smiling and gracious, stood under the rose archway at the side of the drive which formed the entrance to the gardens, so that their guests, whether they came on wheels or on foot, could perceive them at once.

The school-children were to have their tea under the trees in the park, superintended by Meddling Matilda and Clumsy Caroline, but Mr Chubb had thoughtfully provided two tents for their elders – a very large one for the villagers and a much smaller one for the gentry. As the tents were pitched on opposite sides of the rhododendron shrubbery, each was out of sight of the other, and Careless Charles received instructions from his father to stand at the cross way of the two paths leading to these opposite goals, and to invite the ladies and gentlemen coming to the garden-party to go to the right, and the villagers arriving for the beanfeast to the left. But unfortunately, mistaking his father's directions, Charles did exactly the contrary.

Thus the smaller tent, in which only the lightest afternoon tea had been provided, was overcrowded with hungry and discontented villagers, while the larger tent, overflowing with substantial provisions, was but sparsely occupied by the Woolaways, the three Misses Pitt, the Admiral and his wife, Sir Jeremy Wandle, and one or two neighbours with whom the Chubb family were even less well acquainted.

Selfish Cissie and Greedy George, according to their instructions, were zealously handing plates to their visitors, and urging them to eat as much as they could.

'Very extraordinary notions Mr and Mrs Chubb seem to have of entertaining their guests,' said the eldest Miss Pitt, who had been warmly invited by George to take tea or beer, whichever she preferred.

'Well, well,' said the Admiral, busy with a large plateful of cold beef which he was good-naturedly trying to eat rather than disappoint Cissie, who had pressed it upon him, assuring him that there was plenty more where that came from. 'I dare say they haven't much experience yet of giving garden-parties. They are doing their best, poor things, and there's an end of it.'

'I must say I could wish the cups were a little thinner,' said Mrs Woolaway. 'I am so sensitive about china.'

'No plum-pudding, thank you,' said the Admiral's wife, firmly resisting Molly's endeavour to thrust a wedge of cold pudding under her nose. 'I do not take pudding at afternoon tea.'

'Thank you, no veal and ham pie for me. Yes, I've no doubt it's excellent, but I never touch anything solid at this time of day,' said Sir Jeremy rather testily, for he had already been approached with helpings of brawn and pressed beef and sausage-roll.

'Then what will you have?' persisted Cissie. 'Would you like some good strong soup? Papa particularly ordered some to be made for the people whose teeth were not equal to meat.'

At this juncture Mr Chubb happily bustled into the tent with General Finch.

'Tea or beer?' inquired George, at once advancing with a jug and a tumbler.

Mr Chubb looked round distractedly.

'I think there's been some mistake, sir,' said Golightly, arriving breathless in the entrance. 'The people in the other tent is very much upset. They said they was promised a meat tea, and they don't call two plates of small 'am sangwidges a meat tea. The first lot cleared off all the thin bread and butter and cakes and fruit at a mouthful, and an old lady named Martha Otton was so annoyed because there wasn't no beer that she took and bit a large piece out of one of the egg-shell china teacups. And not a quarter of 'em can get in, sir.'

'Bring them all here at once,' said the unhappy Mr Chubb. 'Bless me, what a painful beginning for our festivities. How Charles can be so careless I can't think. Pray excuse him, ladies. These little ups and downs will occur in a large family.'

The villagers were soon enjoying as substantial a meal as their hearts could desire, while the Admiral and the Mayor, Mrs Plumpton and Mrs Woolaway assisted George and Cissie in waiting upon them, and the General conducted the remainder of Mr Chubb's neighbours to the croquet ground.

Dreamy Dorothea, who had taken charge of the smaller tent, was thus set free from her duties, so she joined Charles and went down to the swings which had been put up for school-children, where they swung Tumbling Teddy to his heart's content until he fell out and bumped his head, when he had to be consoled with toffee and handed over to Nanny, who was sitting on the stump of a tree with a twin on each knee, taking no part in the rejoicings.

Aunt Emily, infected by the joyousness of the occasion, was gaily swinging herself, after distributing buns and oranges to the school-children till they could eat no more.

William had a basket full of packets of peppermint lozenges to give to the old women, and Emily snuff and tobacco for the old men, and both had been exceedingly busy.

'I have given all mine away,' said Emily to Charles. 'I didn't know whether the General was old enough to take snuff, so I asked him, and he said he was; and the Admiral had the last ounce of tobacco. And William gave three screws of peppermint to the oldest Miss Pitt. She was *so* surprised.'

'You little geese, they were for the villagers,' said Charles.

'I know that,' said William stoutly; 'But I thought it very unfair that the villagers should get *all* the peppermint, so I gave the other old ladies their share.'

'I suppose we may eat what's over, ourselves,' said Emily.

As soon as all the refreshments had been distributed the whole gathering assembled on the lawn for the sports, which were to be organised by the Mayor and the Admiral who knew everyone present.

The egg-and-spoon race came first, and Mrs Chubb, surrounded by her friends, took her place at one end of the lawn, beside a large table covered with the expensive prizes promised by Mr Chubb. The winner of this race was to receive a silver clock, and the entries were numerous, including Aunt Emily, who was determined to enjoy herself thoroughly while she was about it.

There was a slight delay before starting, as the eggs had been forgotten, and Clumsy Caroline in bringing the basket across the croquet ground caught her foot in a hoop and broke every one of them, to the great vexation of the players. But a fresh supply of eggs was immediately procured, and a most exciting race ensued. Eggs flew about in every direction, and eventually there was a close finish between Aunt Emily and Joshua Grute, who arrived simultaneously, though the united efforts of the Admiral and the Mayor could not persuade Joshua Grute that he had not won.

'It was a dead heat!' shouted the Admiral in his ear.

'I ain't dead-beat at all,' said the old man indignantly. 'I took my time, or I should have dropped my egg same as the others did. I walked from start to finish as cool as you please; it's the young ones as ran all the way and couldn't bring their eggs in along with them as looks foolish, not me. I knowed I was going to win. I could ha' told you so beforehand. My head is clear and my hand is steady, and all for why? Because I ain't got at the beer barrel like some of my neighbours,' and he looked pointedly at Martha Otton, who was smiling amiably but fatuously at everyone, supported by her grandchild Bella.

'This is very awkward, Thomas,' said Aunt Emily, annoyed. 'We cannot cut the clock in half. What is to be done?'

'It is very simple. You must give up your share of the prize to old Grute, Emily.'

'I don't see that at all, Thomas,' argued Aunt Emily. 'To begin with, a silver clock is a most unsuitable prize for him.'

'Nonsense, Emily. Why should he not enjoy possessing a silver clock as much as anybody else? I detest these distinctions,' said Mr Chubb warmly. 'A clock is a clock.'

'I did not say he would not enjoy it, Thomas,' said Aunt Emily obstinately. 'I said it would be unsuitable, and I say so still. Of course, if you insist upon depriving me of a reward which I have lawfully won, I cannot prevent you. But half the clock is honestly my own. I ran, and I wan – I mean, I won – and nobody can deny it.'

'I am not attempting to deny it, Emily,' said Mr Chubb mildly. 'Nobody who saw you run could ever forget it. I was thunderstruck when I beheld you arrive with the egg safe and sound. And as I am far from wishing to disappoint you, I will write to town for a duplicate of the clock, on condition you allow that worthy old man to take this one away.'

'Thomas, you were ever ready to listen to reason,' said Aunt Emily, pressing his hand, and harmony was immediately restored.

During this dispute the three-legged race was run, and the lawn presently looked almost like a battlefield, for it was strewn with competitors quite unsuited for the struggle, who had been tempted to enter the lists by the value of the prize offered, for Mrs Chubb displayed a pair of solid silver candlesticks.

Joshua Grute, elated by his previous success and unmindful of his age, had allowed himself to be tied by the leg to Golightly, and

now lay groaning in the middle of the course, declaring that his
back was broken; Jones, the head gardener, who had a violent
temper, was on the ground pommelling the second coachman,
whom he accused of deliberately tripping him up; and Mr Higginbotham, who had started leg to leg with Charles in the highest of
spirits, was weeping bitterly over a twisted ankle, caused, as he
declared, by Charles's persistent attempt to run faster than he
could.

'A nice thing for me to bring my husband out to enjoy hisself,
and see him lamed for life,' exclaimed Mrs Joshua Grute resentfully, as she struggled with the knots which bound her partner to
Golightly, who for his part lay smiling on his back without making
the slightest attempt to release himself. 'It serves you right,
Joshua. Why couldn't you be content with one prize, and come
away as I bid you?'

As her husband could not hear a single word of her reproaches,
he did not answer, but as soon as he was released Mrs Chubb
was much relieved to see him scramble up and walk away as
though nothing had happened.

Mr Chubb distributed half-sovereigns among the wounded,
and William and Emily, who had won the prize easily, each took
a candlestick and retired into the background well pleased.

'I think these sports are terribly dangerous, Thomas,' said
Mrs Chubb, when Charles and Dorothea had won a pair of
silver fruit-dishes for the under and over race, and Greedy
George a biscuit-box for running in sacks. 'And I fancy,
besides, that it does not look well for our own children to be
carrying off all the prizes like this. I wish you would think of
something else to do.'

'I am almost worn out with my efforts to please as it is, Maria,'
said poor Mr Chubb; 'but we can leave the villagers to amuse
themselves as they choose now, under the guidance of Mr and
Mrs Woolaway, while we go and look on at the croquet tournament, which will be less agitating, and in which our children cannot win prizes, as they are not playing. To tell you the truth, my
love, I shall not be sorry when this entertainment is over. The
strain upon me has been very great.'

The croquet tournament being ended when they arrived, Mrs
Chubb was just in time to present the prizes, which she did with

much grace. The Admiral's wife and the General were the joint winners, and were consequently in high good-humour, one receiving a silver rose-bowl and the other a gold-mounted tortoiseshell paper-knife. The three Misses Pitt were also radiant, for they received the second, third and consolation prizes, consisting of an inkstand, a photograph frame and a scent-bottle, all made of silver.

Everybody now began to talk of departure, and Mr Chubb could not resist the chance thus offered him of making the short speech he had composed for the occasion.

'Friends and neighbours!' he cried, suddenly mounting a garden-chair, and waving his hand for silence, 'I take this opportunity of assuring you of my lively gratitude for past favours . . .'

'Thomas, you are talking like an advertising circular,' said Aunt Emily in a loud whisper.

'Be silent, Emily,' said Mr Chubb in a vexed aside. '. . . and my determination to inaugurate a series of entertainments equal in every way to the one we have just enjoyed. I am a plain but hearty man, and I offer you a plain and hearty welcome. I hope you will gather round me in this informal manner again next summer. I have no more to say but to bid you . . .'

No one ever knew what Mr Chubb was about to bid his neighbours, for the chair upon which he stood, being placed on a slight incline, suddenly tipped forward, and he would have fallen flat upon his face had it not been that Aunt Emily, against whom he fell, sustained him by her weight. He was momentarily disconcerted, but the Admiral's wife now advanced and shook his hand warmly.

'I am sure I, for one, shall be delighted to come next year, Mr Chubb,' she said cheerfully.

'So shall I,' said Martha Otton, smiling more foolishly than ever.

'You won't be alive next year, Granny, unless you give up your bad ways,' said Bella severely; but she too was smiling, for she had won a gold brooch in a threading-the-needle race.

At last the beanfeast came to an end, though it outlived the garden-party by nearly two hours, and the Chubb family, fatigued by their exertions, but in excellent spirits, were able to retire to the house and make ready for their evening meal.

At dessert Mr Chubb begged the General to give a more particular account of the family treasure to which he had alluded during his stay at the castle.

'I have been thinking the matter over carefully,' said Mr Chubb, 'and as I have been all over every corner of the mansion, with the exception of the roof, I do not see how it could have escaped my observation, unless it is very small.'

'Nobody knows its size or what it consists of,' replied the General, 'but several of the old Finch papers allude mysteriously to the time when a great discovery will be made by a member of the family. It is supposed that the treasure was hidden in the reign of Queen Elizabeth, when our ancestor, Sir Jasper de Fynche, went to Spain, and returned with a quantity of booty which was never accounted for, and which he was supposed to have won at play from an unfortunate young Spanish hidalgo. His descendants searched for it in vain.'

'Then we really *have* a romantic family history?' said Dorothea, enchanted.

'I am glad you did not mention it before the servants, for it might have put it into their heads to go hunting about for it,' said Mr Chubb.

'What if they did, Thomas,' said Aunt Emily, 'since only a member of the Finch family can find it?'

'Emily, do not be foolishly superstitious,' said Mr Chubb.

'Could we not search for it by moonlight in the vaults below?' said Dorothea, clasping her hands. 'Oh, Father, 'twould be thrilling indeed.'

'No, Dorothea; I have had quite enough of groping about in the cellars in the middle of the night,' said Mr Chubb hastily. 'We will start tomorrow and search the roof thoroughly. There are quantities of hiding-places there, I believe.'

'I can't see what we want any more treasures for,' said Mrs Chubb mournfully. 'I live in constant terror as it is of things getting broken and spoilt. I felt much more at my ease at home, where there was nothing that mattered.'

'At the rate you and Thomas are living – entertaining the whole county, and giving a silver clock to every labourer who chooses to run for it – I should say you would want as many treasures as you can get,' said Aunt Emily.

'*I* won nothing at all,' said Mr Higginbotham dismally. 'Not so much as a silver button-hook.'

'I should hope not,' said Miss Jenkins severely. 'What does a young man like you want with silver button-hooks, I should like to know?'

13

THE BURGLAR

Bedtime came at last, and the members of the Chubb family were
not sorry to retire to their respective pillows; but Dorothea's
romantic nature had been so deeply stirred by the allusion to her
adventurous ancestor, that she thought of him incessantly, and fell
asleep only to dream of Sir Jasper de Fynche and the treasure he
had brought over from Spain. This caused her to wake in the
middle of the night with one of her sudden inspirations, and after
much thought she produced the following lines:

> *Beetle-browed, bandy-legged, brawling old forbear of mine,*
>   *Thee I do sternly adjure.*

Where in this ivy-clad, secret-staired mansion of thine,
Secretly didst thou immure

Treasure thou reftst from the swarthy-faced Spaniard of yore?
I, thy descendant, would fain
Unto the heir of that noble hidalgo restore
That which thou foully didst gain.

Being unable for the moment to think of anything more to add to this appeal to the shade of her gambling ancestor, Dorothea determined to write it down while she remembered it, so she jumped out of bed and pulled up the blind, observing by the moonbeams which found their way through the chinks of the curtain that there would be quite enough light for her to write by. As she did so, however, her blood ran cold in her veins, for she perceived a figure clad in white slowly crossing the stretch of moonlit grass before her window.

Dorothea was for a moment too terrified to move; then she caught up her dressing-gown and fled barefooted from her room to that of Charles, which was exactly opposite.

She had some difficulty in waking her brother, for he slept very soundly, but after she had shaken him for a moment he jumped up and asked what was the matter.

'Charles,' whispered Dorothea hurriedly, 'wake up! Sir Jasper de Fynche is walking in the garden just under my window.'

'Who?' said Charles, astonished.

'Our ancestor, who brought the treasure from Spain,' said Dorothea, 'or rather his ghost.'

'Pooh!' said Charles.

'If you don't believe me, come and see for yourself,' said Dorothea indignantly. 'He is dressed all in white, and is carrying something in his hand – no doubt the treasure.'

'Go and keep an eye upon him while I get some clothes on,' said Charles. 'I won't be a second.'

Dorothea was too romantic to be cowardly, so she braced up her nerves and went back to her room, where she perceived that the figure was wandering up and down in the moonlight, and she rushed back to tell Charles that he was still visible.

Charles was now partially dressed, and he stole across the

passage and looked out of Dorothea's window to see for himself who was there.

'As I thought, it's a burglar,' he said excitedly. 'He is dressed up in white to make the family believe he's a ghost, but his bag of tools betrays him. I must say it was very plucky of you, Dolly, to come quietly and wake *me*, instead of screaming the house down as some girls might have done. Now we shall have the credit of catching him all to ourselves.'

Dorothea was firmly convinced that the supposed burglar was a spectre, but she had not been brought up with three brothers without having learnt the uselessness of attempting to argue with a boy, so she merely asked Charles what he proposed to do.

'You can't shoot him, even if he's real, Charles,' she said, 'for Papa has locked up the gun-room.'

'Yes, and this just shows the folly of not having fire-arms handy,' said Charles. 'In a house like this everyone should know where to lay his hand on a loaded revolver. As it is, I must do the best I can without weapons. But I will call strategy to my aid. I shall take one of the big sacks we used in the sports today.'

'They are all heaped under the staircase with the croquet mallets and lots of other things,' siad Dorothea.

'I know. And I shall go softly up behind him and throw it over his head.'

'If I stepped suddenly forth into the moonlight and uttered a wild piercing cry, wouldn't that startle him and make it easier for you?' said Dorothea.

'It might,' said Charles doubtfully; 'but I don't like your being in it at all. You're only a girl, and you might get hurt.'

'I may be only a girl, but I'm two years older than you are,' said Dorothea warmly; 'and I certainly won't be kept out of it. Remember, I might have called Papa and not you!'

'That's true,' said Charles. 'I suppose it *would* be rough luck on you, but you must let me do the fighting.'

'All right, I only want to be there,' said Dorothea. 'Besides, if it's really a ghost after all – how would you like to be out of doors all alone with it?'

'Pooh!' said Charles, affecting a contempt he was far from feeling.

All this time they had been creeping cautiously downstairs in the moonlight, and Charles was presently searching among the *débris* of the sports, from whence he drew a large sack and some long cords, but not without upsetting the box of croquet mallets and making a considerable noise.

'Come on, before anyone else wakes,' he whispered, and they unlocked the side door as quietly as possible and stole out into the garden.

The night was so hot as to be almost oppressive, and the harvest moon shone serenely in the sky, making the lights and shadows extraordinarily distinct.

The two children crept along side by side in the shade of the house, Charles carrying the sack and Dorothea the cords. As they came round the corner they beheld the figure again quite clearly. It was groping with one hand as if feeling its way, though the moon was so bright, and presently it dropped on its knees and began grubbing in a flower-bed.

'Charles, it is Sir Jasper, and he's burying the treasure in the earth,' whispered Dorothea, shivering.

'Rot!' said Charles, but he held her hand rather tightly.

'Listen, he's groaning,' said Dorothea, and a moaning sound was distinctly audible.

'He's stealing the geraniums, that's what he's doing,' said Charles. 'He's pulled up two and stuffed them into his bag. A ghost wouldn't do that. Look, he's in a splendid attitude now, sitting up on his heels. I could creep up behind him and throw the sack over his head in a moment.'

'Very well,' said Dorothea. 'If he's a ghost of course he'll vanish as soon as you get near him, but at any rate we shall know where to look for the treasure.'

They then emerged from the shadows and went swiftly across the moonlit grass until they were close behind the ghost.

Charles, forgetting his fright in his anxiety to trap his prey, then deftly flung the sack over his victim's head and shoulders, and throwing his arms round the figure, rolled over with it on to the ground.

The victim kicked and struggled so violently that it became evident even to Dorothea that he was no ghost, and she came to her brother's assistance boldly, winding the cords round and round the burglar in spite of his muffled shrieks, until their united efforts made him fast, when Charles ordered him to be silent, and they both sat down upon his prostrate form to consult upon their next action in the matter.

Meantime Mr Chubb, who was a light sleeper, had been disturbed by the noise of the falling croquet mallets in the hall, and awaking his wife as gently as he could, confided to her his fear that there were thieves in the house. Mrs Chubb immediately forgot her own terror in her alarm for the safety of her beloved twins, so she went quietly up to the nursery and called the servants, while Mr Chubb seized the poker and stole downstairs to reconnoitre.

He discovered almost at once that the side door was open, and hastily throwing on a cloak which hung on a peg behind it, he stepped out of doors, keeping cautiously close to the house, as the children had done.

Aunt Emily meanwhile had also been awakened by the noise in the hall, and lost not an instant in locking herself into her room. She then opened her window and leaned out as far as she could to see what she could see. What was her horror to discover the cloaked figure of a man lurking in the shadow immediately beneath her window. With great presence of mind she flew to her washstand, and emptied the whole contents of the water-jug over the intruder, screaming 'Stop thief!' as loudly as she could at the same time.

Poor Mr Chubb, between the shock and the cold douche, lost both his breath and his balance, and fell backwards into a bed of hollyhocks with a gasp of dismay. The General, hearing Aunt Emily's screams through the wall, leaped out of bed and threw open his window, and perceiving Charles and Dorothea sitting on the prostrate form of the burglar in the moonlight, called out to know what the matter was.

'It's a burglar!' shouted Charles. 'Dorothea and I have caught him, and I am sitting on his head in case he should try to get away. It's all right.'

'It's not all right,' screamed Aunt Emily, 'for there is a second burglar hiding among the hollyhocks.'

Poor Mr Chubb rose indignantly.

'Don't attempt to move, man, or I will shoot you without mercy!' cried Aunt Emily, pointing a hair-brush at him, which she hoped he would mistake in the dark for a pistol.

'Don't be absurd, Emily!' roared Mr Chubb, losing all patience.

'Is it you, Thomas?' said Aunt Emily, aghast.

'Of course it is,' said Mr Chubb crossly. 'Common sense might have told you I should come to the rescue of my children. You have wet me through and through.'

The General, followed by Golightly and several of the other servants, now rushed round the corner of the house armed with sticks and lanterns, and Charles and Dorothea, still sitting upon the burglar, were surrounded.

'Form yourselves into a hollow square,' said the General in a voice of command, and the servants obeyed him without having the least idea what he meant. 'Come round closer, men, in case he should try to escape. Now, Charles and Dorothea, when I say "Ready," get up.'

Far from trying to escape, the burglar lay perfectly motionless.

'He may be shamming. Take care! Burglars are very artful,' said Mr Chubb warningly.

'He's more probably half suffocated,' said the General. 'Take off the sack, men, and give him air.'

As the sack was removed, the burglar sat up and wept bitterly.

'It's Mr Higginbotham!' said Charles, horror-struck at perceiving the well-known features of his tutor.

'Charles and Dorothea, what does this mean?' said their father, wrapping himself up in the sack and looking sternly at them.

'Ask *him* what it means!' said Charles, indignantly. 'What was he doing at this time of night, pulling up the geraniums and putting them into his bag?'

'I dreamt I was packing up my little bag and going on a journey,' sobbed Mr Higginbotham.

'I think it more than probable that your dream will be realised, unless you can offer a satisfactory explanation of your conduct, sir,' said Mr Chubb.

'I must have been walking in my sleep; it is a habit to which I am unfortunately liable,' said poor Mr Higginbotham, weeping more profusely than ever. 'And I ought not to have been wakened suddenly. It is highly dangerous. My aunt never permitted it. Yet I was savagely attacked in the very middle of my dream, and woke to find myself almost smothered beneath a haavy weight.'

'I am very sorry for you, Mr Higginbotham, but I think in

common fairness to me you ought to have mentioned your habit,' said Mr Chubb stiffly. 'In my present condition I cannot go into the question as fully as could be wished, but tomorrow morning . . .'

'Thomas, you will catch your death of cold, and it will lie at my door!' shrieked Aunt Emily.

'You mean at your window, Emily,' replied Mr Chubb, and being much pleased at his own ready wit, he ceased to lecture Mr Higginbotham, and hastened into the house, where, after bolting the door safely behind them, the whole party retired to their respective rooms.

Mrs Chubb was dismayed to perceive the drenched condition of her spouse, and administered every remedy she could think of to prevent his catching cold.

'I am growing very tired of Finch Hall, Thomas,' she said with a sigh. 'What with beanfeasts in the afternoon and burglars in the evening, there seems to be no rest for either of us, day or night.'

'I cannot deny that I am hourly tempted to regret my regular work in the City and the peacefulness of our suburban retreat,' replied Mr Chubb, 'but duty is duty, and never shall it be said that Thomas Chubb failed to realise the fact.'

14

THE GREAT DISCOVERY

At eleven o'clock next morning Mr Chubb desired his whole family to assemble in the library, that he might issue his directions as to the manner in which the search for the missing treasure was to be conducted.

'You, Maria,' he said, 'not being strong enough to go roaming about the house, will remain quietly where you are, upon the sofa, while I explore the roof, or perhaps I should say, the unoccupied topmost attics and chambers of the roof, to supervise the exertions of my children, and to make sure that in their very natural zeal to make the great discovery we anticipate, they do not come to any harm or do any damage.'

'What is to be done with the treasure when we *do* find it, Thomas?' said Aunt Emily suddenly. 'Before risking my neck on the roof I insist upon knowing whether I am to get my share. I will not be made into a cat's-paw unawares.'

'I have already thought this question out very carefully, Emily,' replied Mr Chubb, with unfailing dignity, 'but I cannot make up my mind whether the finder ought to claim the largest share, or whether all the descendants of Sir Jasper de Fynche (for I count my beloved Maria and myself as one) ought to divide the treasure equally between them, irrespective of the actual finder, who may just as well be little Teddy as the General or yourself, Emily, for that matter.'

'It will certainly not be Teddy,' cried Mrs Chubb, in alarm, 'for he must be left with me. I will not let him go climbing about on the roof, treasure or no treasure.'

'As you have eleven children, Thomas, if each of them is to have a share, and you and Maria count as one – you then practically secure twelve-fourteenths of the whole for yourself,' said Aunt Emily, who had been busily making calculations in her notebook. 'This appears to me to be unjust.'

'But on the other hand, as your brother Thomas is lord of the manor, I believe that he could claim the whole,' argued the General. 'In which case his offer is a very generous one, Cousin Emily.'

Mr Chubb grasped the General's hand.

'Your remark does equal credit to your head and your heart, Cousin Benjamin,' he said, with emotion, 'though, since I possess a perfectly balanced mind, I confess that I am much struck by the force of Emily's objection. I have no desire to keep the treasure all to myself.'

'I don't believe you can, Father, if it's treasure trove. It says in my almanac . . .' said William.

'William, when we desire to hear the contents of your almanac we will ask for them,' said his father majestically.

'But the Government takes . . .'

'Be silent, William! I am well aware what the Government takes,' said Mr Chubb angrily. 'Maria, have you any suggestion to bring forward?'

'You know I never make suggestions, Thomas,' said his wife, much flurried by this appeal. 'If I suggested anything, it would be that you should all go about your usual occupations and give up thinking of any such nonsense. Hunting for treasure will just end in your falling through trap doors or down secret staircases and killing yourselves, and where will be the advantage of that?'

'Maria, this pessimism is ridiculous,' said Mr Chubb. 'However, the discussion has nevertheless borne useful fruit. For in hearing the opinions of others alone are we able to recognise the strength and superiority of our own views. I wish to be at the same time just and generous, and I therefore propose that the treasure (when found) should be divided into three portions, one portion for each generation here represented. Thus the General, who represents the oldest living generation of Finches, will receive one portion; Maria and Emily, who represent the next, will divide the second portion between them; and my eleven children will each take an equal share of the third. I believe, Cousin Benjamin, that I have solved the problem.'

The General, with tears in his eyes, declared that nothing could be fairer, and he wrung Mr Chubb's hand again and again.

Mr Chubb begged him not to mention it, but in vain. The General continued to thank him, and the scene became so affecting that Mrs Chubb burst into tears.

'This is all very fine, but we haven't found the treasure yet, nor are we even certain that it exists,' said Aunt Emily. 'I therefore propose that before thanking each other any more we begin the hunt at once.'

The General, somewhat disconcerted, but forced to admire Aunt Emily's common sense in spite of himself, seconded her proposition, and the whole party, with the exception of Mrs Chubb and Teddy, then left the study and mounted to the top floor of Finch Hall.

At Aunt Emily's suggestion, everyone tied up his or her head in a pocket-handkerchief to keep the dust out, and carried a stick; and thus equipped, they climbed the short ladder from the top landing to the trap door which led to the empty spaces beneath the roof, which, as Mr Chubb had truly said, was the only portion of the building he had not already explored.

They found themselves in a *grenier* on a boarded platform

especially designed to hold the large cistern which stood in the middle, beneath a skylight. The rest of the space between the roof and the ceilings of the servants' attics was almost dark, and bats and cobwebs innumerable clung to the mighty beams and rafters above their heads.

'I will go in front in case of mishap, and lead the way,' said Mr Chubb.

'Nonsense, my dear cousin, nonsense!' said the General warmly. 'You are a married man with eleven children, while I am a bachelor. It is clearly my place to lead,' and he stepped lightly off the platform on to the nearest joist.

'I too have no family ties,' said Aunt Emily firmly. 'Where you lead, Cousin Benjamin, I follow. Tread carefully, children; you will soon get used to the semi-twilight. Already I can see quite plainly where I am going.'

This was all very well, but as Aunt Emily had no idea that the spaces between the joists were not as solid as an ordinary floor, she stepped off the beam and on to the lath and plaster with perfect confidence, and the lath and plaster naturally gave way beneath her very considerable weight.

The astonished children saw their aunt sink suddenly down under their very eyes, until only her outstretched arms and terrified face were visible, surrounded by a heap of drapery.

'Emily, what has happened to you?' cried Mr Chubb, in agony.

'I cannot tell you, Thomas,' gasped Aunt Emily. 'The floor appeared to give way, and I can only say that I seem to be treading on air.'

'You must have gone through the ceiling of one of the servants' bedrooms,' said Mr Chubb. 'I will go down at once and ascertain where the rest of you is.'

'Thomas, you will do nothing of the kind!' shrieked Aunt Emily. 'If you and Cousin Benjamin will each take an arm, you can pull me up again.'

Before Mr Chubb and the General had time to carry out this suggestion, a loud muffled scream followed by hysterical laughter, announced that someone had entered the attic below.

'It is Molly,' said Matilda. 'Leave it all to me, Aunt Emily. I will go down and help her push you up.'

But at this moment Aunt Emily, unable longer to sustain her

own weight, relaxed her hold of the joists she was clinging to on either side, and disappeared altogether through the gap in the ceiling.

Fortunately, Molly's feather-bed, on a comfortable wire-wove mattress, stood immediately below the opening, and as Aunt Emily was very well covered she sustained no injury beyond the shock of her own rebound, which was so violent that it almost sent her up to the ceiling again.

'Lord! miss, I shall never forget my surprise when I came in and saw your elastic-sided boots and white stockings kicking in the air over my 'ead,' said Molly, still giggling.

'Your tendency towards excessive mirth, Molly, always misplaced, is more so than ever upon this occasion,' said Aunt Emily severely.

'You bounced like an indiarubber ball, miss,' said Molly admiringly.

After a moment's rest, Aunt Emily announced to the anxious inquirers above that she felt able to rise and rejoin the treasure seekers. Assisted by the General, she once more climbed the ladder to the roof, and this time was careful to tread only upon the stout oak cross-beams, which though centuries old were still sound at heart and enormously strong.

Not a nook nor a cranny was left unvisited as the party moved slowly from one division of the roof into another, sometimes being obliged to crawl on hands and knees, and sometimes emerging into wide spaces beneath lofty rafters, well lighted by interstices among the tiles.

'There's a small door in the wall here, Father,' squeaked sharp little Emily, who always managed to get to the front with William.

'It looks like a manhole,' said William. 'May I get inside?'

'No, sir. Stand aside, children. It really *does* look like the opening to some secret hiding place,' said Mr Chubb breathlessly.

Much excited, he pulled open the door and thrust his head and shoulders inquisitively into the aperture. A shower of soot immediately descended upon him, and he sneezed violently and withdrew in an almost unrecognisable condition.

'You look like a chimney-sweep, Papa,' said Cissie.

'Who cares for a little soot?' said Charles scornfully, and followed his father's example.

'It is merely an opening into a chimney,' said Mr Chubb, much annoyed.

'Treasures have been hidden in chimneys before now,' said Dorothea warningly.

'It's not an ordinary chimney, Papa,' said Charles. 'Now my eyes are used to the light, I can see there are steps cut in the side and handles sticking out all the way down. It is a regular staircase, and there are great beams going right across it, and it gets wider and wider. Anybody could climb it.'

'Charles, come down instantly. Let me look,' said Mr Chubb. 'Bless me, this is very extraordinary. Depend upon it, this was a way of escape especially designed in the olden time for hunted fugitives. There may be some secret chamber to which access is only obtainable through this channel. It is my duty to leave no stone unturned, and I shall take the descent upon myself.'

'Thomas – run no risks, I beseech you! Think of Maria!' screamed Aunt Emily.

'I don't believe you will be able to get through the opening, Papa,' said William, measuring his parent's girth with his eye. 'I am almost sure you will stick.'

'William, your assurance is to me little short of amazing,' said Mr Chubb indignantly. 'As a punishment you will retrace your footsteps and join your mother in the library. You are not worthy, sir, to make a discovery of any sort.'

'He didn't mean it, Papa,' said Emily in a hurry; 'did you, William?'

'Yes, I did,' said William, offended. 'I never say what I don't mean. 'I've got my foot-rule in my pocket, and it . . .'

'William!' thundered his father. 'Leave us, without another word.'

Poor William marched away across the joists, and Emily went hopping and skipping after him until they both disappeared into the darkness.

'Charles, give me a leg up,' said Mr Chubb; and he was hoisted into the aperture by the united efforts of the General, Aunt Emily, and Charles, and began cautiously to squeeze himself through the doorway, having previously removed his coat.

For a moment it seemed as though William's prophecy must be fulfilled, so exactly did Mr Chubb's body fit the opening in the chimney. Then a sound like the plop of a cork was heard, and he was safely through.

'My feet are on the step and I am holding on by a beam and a handle,' he said in stifled tones. 'There will not be the slightest difficulty, I fancy, in descending, for it grows wider down below.'

'Keep your eyes fixed on the opening at the top, or you will grow giddy and fall,' cried Aunt Emily. 'What are we to do, Thomas?'

'Go to the library and await my return,' said Mr Chubb, his voice growing fainter and fainter. 'I fancy it is easier to go down than it would be to come up.'

'Nothing will induce me to move until you are safe at the bottom,' shouted Aunt Emily. 'When you see your way out give three whoops, and we will leave our post. Not before.'

After what seemed a long interval three faint halloos announced the safety of Mr Chubb, and Aunt Emily, the General, and the children, who had now practically explored the whole of the roof, all hastened to retrace their footsteps and to find their way back to the library.

Meantime Mr Chubb, more and more astonished at the immense size of the chimney, at last reached the opening at the other end, and stepping down upon a pile of logs, presented himself suddenly in the servants' hall among his assembled household, who were just sitting down to their early dinner.

Golightly, who was the first to perceive him, uttered a yell of terror and slipped under the table. Molly went into hysterics, and Margery was just about to empty a pail of water over the intruder when she recognised her master's voice and figure.

'Well, sir, how could a body imagine *you* would come down the chimney?' she gasped. 'I wouldn't have believed it, if I hadn't seen it.'

'I suppose, Margery, I have a right to come down my own chimney when I choose,' said Mr Chubb, with the dignity that never deserted him. 'Let me tell you, once for all, that I consider every portion of my household under my direct personal supervision, and that I am liable to appear among you when you least expect it. Golightly, get up at once.'

'Yes, sir,' said Golightly, trembling.

'Why do you not open the door for me?' said Mr Chubb sternly.

'I didn't know but what you might be returning the same way, sir,' stammered Golightly.

'Take a can of hot water to my bedroom without an instant's delay,' said Mr Chubb, and he walked out of the servants' hall without deigning to glance behind him again.

A few minutes later he entered the library once more, having removed all traces of his last adventure from his person, and changed his clothes.

'I regret to tell you, Maria, that everyone has so far been unsuccessful in making any discovery at all,' he said rather mournfully.

'No, they have not, Thomas,' said Mrs Chubb, who was in tears, 'for William has just found a will made by our Cousin Joseph leaving everything away from us to his brother the General.'

Poor Mr Chubb was thunderstruck.

'I came down here, as you told me, Papa,' said William, 'and I sat on the sofa by Mamma, and put my hand down at the back as far as it would go, and pulled out a roll of paper, and here it is. It is dated the day before Cousin Joseph died.'

'This is indeed a remarkable discovery,' said Mr Chubb, reading the paper in dismay.

'My dear Cousin Thomas, you are agitating yourself unnecessarily,' said the General. 'The document is certainly in my poor brother's own handwriting, but if you will turn to the end you will perceive it is unsigned.'

'It is not worth the paper it is written on,' said Aunt Emily, snapping her fingers.

'Never shall it be said, Emily,' said Mr Chubb firmly, 'that a trifling informality of this kind caused Thomas Chubb to cling to an inheritance that did not justly belong to him. Nothing but my conviction that I was acting in accordance with the wishes of our lamented relative induced me to accept his legacy. It is now perfectly clear that his last wishes were that his half-brother should succeed him at Finch Hall. I therefore on behalf of my wife, to whom the property was left unconditionally, cheerfully restore to Cousin Benjamin his lawful inheritance.'

'Do not for a moment suppose I would accept the sacrifice,'

said the General, shaking Mrs Chubb's hand so violently that she could hardly prevent herself from screaming aloud.

'Indeed, Cousin Benjamin, it is no sacrifice so far as I am concerned. I am crying for joy at the thought of getting back to my own comfortable house again, away from this mysterious old place which I am sure is haunted, for the very suits of armour in the hall look half alive, and only last night poor Golightly, through a very natural mistake, offered coffee to one of them; and Thomas owns that his business in the City is going to wrack and ruin without him, while he has nothing to do here from morning till night.'

'I cannot think my poor brother Joseph was in his right mind when he made this will,' expostulated the General. 'You observe he remarks he has just been to a pantomime and seen you surrounded by your family. What was he doing at a pantomime at his age?'

'He must have been in his second childhood,' said Aunt Emily.

'I defy you to find a better reason for going to the pantomime, Emily,' said Mr Chubb warmly.

'Or a worse one for making a will, Thomas,' retorted Aunt Emily.

'Don't dash my hopes to the ground, Emily, just when I was beginning to look forward to returning so happily to the neighbourhood of the Crystal Palace,' entreated Mrs Chubb. 'Thomas and I have never felt really comfortable about owning this property, especially since we have known that Cousin Joseph had a brother.'

'I had hoped to make amends by dividing the treasure,' said Mr Chubb gloomily.

'Let me make a proposition,' said the General, twisting his moustache. 'We anticipated making a discovery . . .'

'A fine discovery it has turned out to be,' said Aunt Emily.

'Without knowing what it would turn out to be, we agreed to divide the results into three equal shares,' said the General. 'I propose that we should abide by that decision.'

'It is an excellent plan,' exclaimed Aunt Emily.

Mr Chubb now in his turn wrung the General's hand.

'Maria shall execute the necessary deeds without a moment's delay,' he cried. 'Your poor brother's fortune shall be divided into three shares – the first, including Finch Hall, as he wished, shall be yours; the second shall be Maria's and Emily's, and the third shall be held by myself in trust for our eleven children. Thus justice will be done to everyone, and we shall all be quite as well off as we have any need to be.'

'Thomas, you are wonderful!' said his wife, with tears of admiration shining in her eyes.

'Mr Chubb, be very sure that your children shall not be the losers by your just and generous action,' said the General, putting one hand on Charles's shoulder and the other on William's.

Everything was arranged in accordance with these plans. Mr Chubb, having now plenty of money, and no country place to keep up, enlarged his business in the City, and grew more interested in it every day.

Mrs Chubb visited the Crystal Palace as often as she chose, found her own house more comfortable than ever, and was very peaceful and happy with her old servants about her, ready and willing to bring her a cup of tea at a moment's notice. Miss Jenkins continued to teach the girls, except selfish Cissie, who was sent to school; and Mr Higginbotham's dream came true, for he had to pack his little bag, and return to his aunt at Putney, when Charles went to Eton, George to Harrow, and William to Osborne.

The General married Aunt Emily and settled down at Finch Hall, and Aunt Emily was very glad to be married; and as she and the General had no children of their own, they were never happy unless their nephews and nieces were staying with them.

Thus the great discovery brought happiness and satisfaction to everybody concerned in it, and there may be plenty of adventures still in store for the Unlucky Family, since the mysterious Finch Treasure has yet to be found.